THE
GARDEN
CLASSROOM

THE
GARDEN
CLASSROOM

Hands-On Activities in Math, Science, Literacy, and Art

CATHY JAMES

Boulder
2015

Roost Books
An imprint of Shambhala Publications, Inc.
4720 Walnut Street
Boulder, Colorado 80301
roostbooks.com

9 8 7 6 5 4 3 2

Printed in the United States of America

♾ This edition is printed on acid-free paper that meets the American National Standards Institute Z39.48 Standard.
♻ Shambhala Publications makes every effort to print on recycled paper. For more information please visit www.shambhala.com.

Distributed in the United States by Penguin Random House LLC and in Canada by Random House of Canada Ltd

Designed by Katrina Noble

Library of Congress Cataloging-in-Publication Data

James, Cathy.
The garden classroom: hands-on activities in math, science, literacy, and art / Cathy James.–First edition.
pages cm
Other title: Hands-on activities in math, science, literacy, and art
ISBN 978-1-61180-164-4 (alk. paper)
1. Gardening for children. 2. Gardening–Study and teaching (Early childhood)–Activity programs. 3. Outdoor education. I. Title. II. Title: Hands-on activities in math, science, literacy, and art
SB457.J36 2015
635.083–dc23
2014006447

For Pamela and Benny Bowes, who know their onions when it comes to growing children.

And for Ken Lightfoot, who helped give me a great start in life.

CONTENTS

Welcome to the Garden Classroom   ix

INTRODUCTION: *Nurturing Young Gardeners*   1

1. LET'S GROW! GARDEN BASICS   11

2. PLAY & IMAGINATION   53

3. READING & WRITING   81

4. SCIENCE & MATH   105

5. ARTS & CRAFTS   145

6. GARDEN RECIPES   189

Garden Journal   199

Resources   217

Join the Garden Classroom Community   221

About the Author   222

WELCOME TO THE GARDEN CLASSROOM

A garden classroom is such a wonderful place to spend time during your childhood. Whether you have a plot of ground growing vegetables or simply a few plant pots, whether there is a lawn or a hard-surfaced yard, any space where you are growing plants, and playing and learning outdoors, can be included within the concept of a garden classroom. Every garden—from the smallest container garden to a giant vegetable plot—offers children a rich sensory playground full of interesting things to discover and learn about: There's a whole lot of science happening right before their eyes. They're surrounded by nature's art, with the gallery changing from season to season. There's space to run free, build forts, and play. The garden can also be a place to develop math and literacy skills, as the outdoors offers plenty of invitations to weave learning into your everyday gardening. For more formal learning, you'll find that anything you want to study in a traditional indoor classroom can be learned as well, if not better, outdoors. The garden classroom is a place where plants grow and children grow too.

I'm passionate about children and gardening. From my own children, my work with preschoolers, and the school gardening club that I ran, I've seen many times the benefits kids get from being close to nature. Your garden, no matter its size, is an outdoor classroom waiting to be explored, and this book is bursting with ideas you can use to make the most of the science, art, and learning that's waiting for you outside your back door.

My own garden is a tiny city space. We have no lawn, but beautiful Victorian walls give us a sheltered spot. With limited space, we need to maximize everything we have, and we manage to combine areas for play, relaxing, and learning as well as for more than thirty different varieties of fruit, vegetables, and herbs. If you're not much of a gardener yourself, or even if you have no garden at all, this book still has lots of ideas for you to try so your children can reap the benefits of a garden classroom, whether it's your own or the local park or a woodland.

All the ideas in this book have been tried, tested, and approved by children. A few are more suited to toddlers and some are better for older children, but the majority are adaptable to your child's age, stage, and interests. *The Garden Classroom* brings you a whole year's worth of garden projects. Come rain or shine, and whatever the season, there are ideas you can use to give children a connection to nature all year-round. You can group ideas together if you're homeschooling, planning a class project, or looking for ideas for the summer break, or you can dip into the book and try a different idea each week. You'll find tips on what to grow with children and how to get started as well as suggestions for science studies you can try. There are lots of art and craft projects and ideas that will take math, literacy, and imaginary play outside.

I hope you and your children enjoy the ideas in *The Garden Classroom*.

— Cathy

INTRODUCTION
Nurturing Young Gardeners

Anything you can teach in an indoor classroom can be taught outdoors, often in ways that are more enjoyable for children. Working in a garden cements the learning in real hands-on, practical experiences and brings lessons back to being stimulating and fun. In addition, a garden classroom offers extra elements that cannot be so easily found in an indoor school.

A richly varied curriculum. The garden itself provides an engaging and evolving curriculum, guiding your lesson planning as you follow the natural progress of the seasons through the year. Simply following the cycle of planting seeds, nurturing and observing their growth, and harvesting their produce gives you a complete science study, as you will see in the Sunflowers section starting on page 112. The garden also offers an interesting selection of natural materials that are readily available and free of cost. We'll see later in the book how items such as seeds, flowers, twigs, and even mud can be used as sensory resources, manipulatives for math and literacy work, inspiration for creative writing, and materials for arts and crafts. As you garden with your children, you will also see how the outdoor environment is a place that naturally encourages teamwork, bestows the feeling of pride and satisfaction from growing accomplishments, and builds community.

The environment as the third teacher. There is a theory in the Reggio Emilia philosophy of education that along with the child and the teacher, the environment in which we learn plays a role as the third teacher. Perhaps more than anywhere else, we can see this most clearly in a garden classroom.

Taking lessons outdoors can really benefit children who find a classroom environment difficult and help them find enjoyable ways to learn important skills. For some a classroom is a place where you are expected to sit still; where the surroundings are filled with distracting posters, word walls, and information; where learning feels like hard work; and where tests make you nervous. A garden classroom can be the true opposite of this, making it a relaxing, enjoyable place to learn. Away from overwhelming noises or visuals, we can be soothed by the natural surroundings, which can help us focus on the activity we're working on without distraction. There's space to run freely, to exercise our bodies and fidget while at the same time taking part in games, projects, and activities that are full of rich learning. There's a ready supply of natural materials that can be used as rich sensory manipulatives—small items such as leaves and pebbles, which are easily handled by children and can be used in play and as an aid to learning. And as we plant, harvest, and play, real-life, valuable lessons are weaving through all that we do, making the learning robust but satisfyingly different from classroom work sheets and testing.

The gift of a connection to nature. More and more of our life is spent in unnatural environments. The children in your class may move daily from home to car to indoor schoolroom to car and back inside a house again. We rise at the same time every day, using artificial lights to stay up long after nightfall, following the same treadmill routine throughout the year. Certainly in a city, or even a suburb, it's possible to run the cycle of a year scarcely noticing the change of seasons. But we are, in our core, natural creatures.

The human race is a people tied to the land. For thousands of years we have lived in and with our natural environment, following the *natural* rhythms of the year, planning our daily routines to match the seasons. It is something we are now losing but something that we have the opportunity to offer back to our children. I think this reconnection to nature is the biggest benefit to be had from taking our learning out into a garden classroom. It's not as discernible as some of the math, science, and literacy learning that is taking place, but it is fundamental. You have the chance to plant a seed of something very special in the hearts, minds, and spirits of your children as you garden together. Whether you call it natural or essential or peaceful or spiritual, it is a strong and compelling motivation to focus your play and learning outdoors.

ORGANIZING YOUR GARDEN CLASSROOM

Let's think now about some practicalities that can help you make the most of your time outdoors and benefit more deeply from the activities in this book. When you are organizing your garden space and planning your curriculum, you'll need to consider the following aspects.

SPACE

It truly doesn't matter how much space you have available; as much can be achieved in even a few pots and containers as in a larger garden. If space is limited, my five favorite plants, which I share in chapter 1, "Let's Grow! Garden Basics," will be useful in helping you maximize what you have. Whatever space is available to you, it is a good idea to spend time planning what you hope to grow, and where, before the first seed packet is opened. The next section, What to Grow with Children (page 5), will help you make choices that suit your circumstances. It is a good idea to dedicate a particular section of your garden or school yard to your outdoor classroom. Perhaps mark it with a special boundary or a gate or decorative entrance, or hang up a welcome sign. This gives your space a reverence and marks a transition from elsewhere into your special garden.

CLOTHING

When you're working out in the elements, you do need to consider clothing. You might have each child provide his or her own apron, raincoat, sun hat, and boots, or have a communal collection that can be used as necessary. Whichever way you organize, keep the clothing readily accessible so you can quickly and easily have all the children outfitted and ready to work whenever you have the opportunity to head outdoors. Think, too, about yourself: you're likely to spend less time running around than the children, so you may be more prone to feel the cold. I find that making sure I am warm and happy means we all spend more time, more enjoyably, outdoors.

SHELTER

Given the right clothing, you can be outdoors in all but extreme weather. Having some shelter available can help you benefit from your outdoor space all year-round. Think about how you might include a shed, a canopy, a fort, or a fire pit in your space to provide a community hub.

TIME

How much time you spend in your garden classroom will be something for you to decide according to your intentions, requirements, and other commitments. You might follow the example of forest schools and spend every single day outdoors. You might focus your garden project mainly within one school term—most likely spring or summer. The garden can be run very well as a lunchtime or after-school club, with children joining you for an hour once a week. Think also about whether you will have a whole class in your garden at any one time or whether you will work with smaller groups.

OBTAINING RESOURCES

How much equipment and funding you have available is an important consideration, but you can get started on an effective garden classroom for very little cost. Think about reusing and recycling as much as you can, and repurpose containers, as with the quirky ecoplanters on page 30. Ask for donations of practical items as well as money: friends, parents, and neighbors may very well be happy to share seeds, plants, and basic tools with you. You don't need to have everything you'd like before you start your project: always think of your garden as growing and evolving over time. Once you have made a start, you will see how you can self-supply certain things by harvesting your own seeds (page 47) and growing your own fertilizer (page 44). The seeds, plants, and produce you generate can also be sold to raise funds for the following years.

CURRICULUM

This book is full of activities you can use throughout the year, across math, science, literacy, play, and arts and crafts. As you plan when to try each activity, you will see that the natural cycle of the year plays an important role in deciding how your curriculum unfolds. It makes sense to schedule much of the science experimenting in the spring, when you are planting and germinating seeds. Cooking activities will fit best later in the summer, when you have produce to harvest and use. Winter months can be a good time to make use of the ideas for indoor arts and crafts. Especially if you have groups of chil-

dren joining your garden club at different times throughout the year, offer a regular mix of activities so every child gets to benefit from a range of pursuits. I find, at any time of year, that the activities of watering, digging, and eating are always the most popular.

WHAT TO GROW WITH CHILDREN

The quick answer to the question of what to grow with children is "Anything." One of the important lessons to be learned from gardening, as a child or an adult, is that we're not totally in charge. We can choose seeds, design a planting scheme, and water correctly, but Mother Nature, as well as a whole host of garden bugs, also has a say. There's an element of risk taking: trying something new to see if it works and picking yourself up again when, after weeks of nurturing, a cheeky snail munches straight through the stem of your prized sunflower. Don't be deterred, though. Use these tips to get your garden off to a great start.

PLAY TO YOUR STRENGTHS

Get to know your garden. How much sunlight do you get? Which areas are always in shade? What's the climate like in your part of the world, and in what period does the growing season fall? Take a peek at neighboring gardens and see what's growing well there. Once you've done a little reconnaissance, play to your advantages. Every garden has great things to offer. A tiny town garden might benefit from the shelter of the surrounding houses and wall. A damp and boggy plot can grow an amazing swamp garden.

CREATE A RIOT FOR THE SENSES

Children are sensory creatures, and using the garden to full effect gives them a paradise to explore. Include lots of flowers for color. Add herbs for scent. Grow fruit and vegetables so they can taste things straight from the plant. Combine a variety of trees, plants, and landscaping so the garden is good to touch. And make wind chimes or include running water for sound.

INVITE WILDLIFE

A garden thrives when it becomes a mini-ecosystem, so do all you can to invite beneficial bugs and birds into your yard. These creatures also give your children a living zoo to investigate and learn about. Flowers with open blooms, such as cosmos and sunflowers, attract pollinating insects. Butterflies love nasturtiums and buddleia. Bird feeders welcome feathered friends.

GROW FOR QUICK RESULTS

Young children like to see things happening, so pick some plants that are quick to produce results. Garden cress, grass seeds, beans, and peas are quick to germinate and grow. Radishes and a cut-and-come-again variety of lettuces provide a tasty harvest without a long wait.

TRY SOMETHING FROM SEED

You might buy some established plants, such as tomatoes and strawberries that are ready to go, but try to grow something from seed each year too. This lets your children follow the cycle of growth and gives them tremendous satisfaction. Harvesting your own seeds in the autumn from plants such as nicotiana and sunflowers teaches children about sustainability.

GO FOR CROWD-PLEASERS

Grow the things children like to eat. You could set up a pizza garden and grow tomatoes, basil, and oregano to make your own toppings. Or try a thornless raspberry bush, cherry tomatoes, or some sugar snap peas so the kids can pick and snack as they play. Add some extras, too; you might find that picky eaters are much more adventurous when they've grown their own veggies.

THROW IN A WILD CARD

Mix things up a little each year by growing something unexpected. Maybe a melon or a grapevine. Perhaps some rainbow-colored carrots or yellow tomatoes. Or see if you can raise your own Halloween pumpkin.

LET KIDS BE HANDS-ON

Let your children have their very own garden bed, or run the garden as a family affair to suit your preference, but do be sure to give the children some opportunity to be hands-on. Some seeds will be dropped and some plants will be overwatered, but take comfort from the knowledge that by letting children join in, you are giving them a beneficial experience that compensates by far for any minor losses. You might like to use the ideas in this book for a fairy garden, an indoor meadow, and a play potting shed to give them a hands-on space of their own (see chapters 1 and 2 for more ideas).

ABOVE ALL, ENJOY!

Things don't always germinate. Slugs will always nibble leaves. Children will often get covered in mud. Relax! The benefits of time in the garden with your children are plentiful. The garden classroom gives space for running around; fresh air for physical and mental health; and a wealth of creative, play, and learning opportunities. So choose some ideas from this book to try, and go enjoy the garden with your children.

———— KEY GARDEN VOCABULARY ————

Annual–A plant that completes its whole life cycle, from germination to seed production, in the space of one year; for example, a sunflower.

Biennial–A plant that completes its whole life cycle, from germination to seed production, in the space of two years; for example, wallflowers.

Compost–Organic matter, such as leaves, vegetable peelings, and grass clippings, that has decomposed to be recycled as a fertilizer and soil improver.

Cotyledons–Not true leaves but the embryonic leaves that appear on a seedling after germination.

Deciduous–A plant that loses its leaves in autumn, winter, or sometimes in a dry season; for example, an oak.

Evergreen–A plant that has leaves in all four seasons, such as a holly or pine.

Germination—The process by which a plant grows from a seed.

Perennial—A plant that lives for more than two years; for example, mint.

Pistil—The seed-producing part of a flower.

Pollination—The transfer of pollen from a stamen to a pistil. Pollination starts the production of seeds and may be carried out by wind, bees, or butterflies.

Repotting—Moving a growing plant to a bigger container to give it more space to mature.

Roots—The part of a plant that usually grows under the soil. Roots are used to anchor and support the plant, collect water, and store nutrients.

Seedling—A young plant that is grown from a seed.

Stamen—The pollen-producing part of a flower.

Stem—The main trunk of a plant.

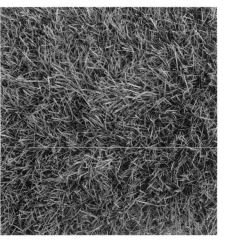

LET'S GROW!
GARDEN BASICS

FRIENDS AND READERS of my blog often tell me they would love to have a garden and grow some of their own food with their children, but they just don't have a green thumb. (Well, actually, here in the UK we say green fingers.) Don't be deterred. No green digits are required because, by and large, it's nature that does all the growing and fruiting and clever stuff. If you can pop a seed into some soil and remember to water it, you're already well on the way to your own productive plot. And if you've managed thus far to raise a child, I'm confident you can raise a garden—with no sleepless nights and no diaper changes to deal with.

In this chapter I'm going to share some tips on getting a garden started. We'll talk about the best things to grow with your children that will make the most of your space for you, the kids, and the wildlife that lives there. I'll suggest five favorite plants to grow, with techniques to help them bloom and encourage them to give you lots of fruit, vegetables, and flowers. We'll look at some practical matters, such as how to plant seeds and keep them well watered. There are also some whimsical projects you can try, to have some fun with what you grow.

FIVE FAVORITE PLANTS TO GROW

When you begin to plan your garden and look at plants to buy or seed packets to purchase, it can feel rather overwhelming. Especially if you are new to this, all the choices available seem to offer lots of potential to get things wrong. So let's keep things really simple to start out. Let's look at five favorite things you could grow with your children this year to get your garden started with success. These plants offer a range of growing experiences: underground, aboveground, vegetables, fruit, and flowers. They're easy to grow and will give you a good chance of raising something your children can pick and eat, all in their first year of gardening. They'll also be able to follow through a full cycle of planting, nurturing, harvesting, and collecting seeds for next year. My favorite picks are potatoes, tomatoes, sunflowers, nasturtiums, and lettuce. If you grew only these five, you'd still have a beautiful, productive garden plot to enjoy through the seasons. Here's how to get the best from each one.

GROWING POTATOES

Potatoes are a great crop to grow with children, and they're also a very good first crop to grow in a garden because they can break up clay soils and improve soil structure generally. They're also a perfect combination to rotate in a spot where you grow peas or beans one year and potatoes the next, because the potatoes will use up the nitrogen introduced into the soil by the peas and beans.

There are many different varieties of potatoes you can grow at home, and when deciding which to buy I always say it's best to think with your tummy. Do your children prefer waxy-type potatoes that are small enough to pop into their mouth in one gulp? In that case, you might try Maris Peer, Charlotte, or Kipfler. For big potatoes with a fluffy texture that you can bake in the oven or use to make fries, go for Maris Piper or King Edward. And try Désirée for perfect mashed potatoes.

Depending on the variety you select, potatoes can be available to harvest from spring to early autumn. And they're so fun to harvest—digging down into the soil to gather the golden potatoes is like pirates digging for treasure.

Planting Potatoes

Buy your seed potatoes early in the year and then allow them to chit before planting them. This simply means setting them in a light, airy spot for a few weeks, until the eyes begin to sprout and you see the first shoots growing upward out of the potato. If you take a look at your potatoes, you'll see that the eyes, or immature shoots, are all at one end, called the rose end. This end needs to be at the top, and setting your potatoes in an egg carton is perfect for chitting. Put one potato in each cavity and write the name of the variety on the egg carton so you don't get mixed up.

Once your potatoes have shoots that are a couple inches long, they're ready to be planted. We always grow our potatoes in containers rather than directly in the soil. This helps to prevent the potatoes from being attacked by pests and diseases, encouraging a better harvest. Using deep containers means we don't have to mound earth around the plants and lets us get a good crop of vegetables in a smaller area of our garden.

Choose a big, deep container. You can buy special potato sacks or use a trash can, an old bathtub, or a basin . . . anything that is sturdy, deep, and not transparent, as it's important that sunlight be kept away from your growing tubers. Make sure there are some drainage holes in the base of your container and fill it with a layer of compost or good garden soil. Make this first layer about eight inches deep and then set your potatoes in the soil with the shooting, rose end upward. Then completely cover the potatoes with more soil, filling the container right up to near the top. Just leave a little room at the top for watering.

Nurturing Your Potatoes

The potato containers are best placed in a sunny spot in the garden and should be watered just enough to keep the compost from drying out.

Harvesting Your Potatoes

As the potatoes in your containers grow, they will produce a crop of potatoes under the soil and send up leaves aboveground. You can check the growing details of the specific variety you have selected, but the time from planting to harvest can be anywhere from ten to twenty weeks. As a general rule, potatoes will usually be ready to harvest after the plants have flowered (although some varieties do not flower at all). If in doubt, dig down for a peek and see how big the potatoes are. Growing your potatoes in containers makes harvesting really easy. You'll just need to upend the pot, and the children can hunt around in the soil to pick out the potato treasures. Be sure to set aside the lovely compost from your containers, using it to fill raised beds elsewhere in the garden or as a mulch (an extra layer on top of the soil to improve the soil and prevent weeds) around other plants. (Have a look at the plant Olympics activity on page 135 for some ideas for math learning that you can combine with your potato harvesting.)

GROWING TOMATOES

A tomato is another plant that grows really well in a container, but you could also pick a tumbling variety to grow in a hanging basket or grow them directly in the ground in your plot. There are many varieties to pick from in a range of shapes, sizes, and colors. One thing they all need is lots of sunshine, so pick your best sunny spot for them to thrive.

Planting Tomatoes

You can grow tomatoes from seed or buy small plants. They're the one thing we seem to struggle to get started from seed, so I would recommend that beginners opt to buy plants for a better chance of a good crop. Check the individual requirements of the variety you've chosen, as some need to be in a greenhouse and others are perfectly happy to be outside. Whichever location you're growing your tomatoes in, use a good-quality compost to give them plenty of nutrients to get off to a strong start.

Nurturing Tomatoes

Tomatoes can be either a bush variety or a vine variety. Vine varieties, such as Gardeners' Delight and Sungold, are grown up a pole, or a length of string. If you look at the stems of the plants as they grow, you'll notice they start to send out little shoots in the

creases between the stalk and the branches. Pinch out these extra side shoots, removing them with your fingers or scissors. This will encourage the plant to concentrate on producing lots of tomatoes for you to eat rather than too much extra foliage. Once your vine tomatoes have produced six or so clusters of tomatoes, snip off the very tops of the plants to keep them from growing any farther. This will help the plant produce a fully ripened crop of tomatoes for you rather than sending all of its energy into taller and taller leafy stems.

Bush varieties of tomatoes (we love Red Alert and Tumbling Tom) can be left to fill out and don't need to have their side shoots removed. All varieties will benefit from being grown alongside French marigolds, which repel whiteflies and attract bees to encourage better pollination.

Tomatoes need regular, even watering—perhaps daily in very hot weather. It's important they're not left to dry out and then given a deluge of water, as this can cause problems with the tomato fruits. It's a job that children can easily help with, and the do-it-yourself watering cans included later in this book are perfect for the job. The plants will also benefit from regular feeding. You can buy a liquid tomato feed, which is often seaweed based, and give it as a weekly supplement with your watering when the plants are beginning to flower and produce tomatoes. You can also make your own feed—take a look at the Garden Power Potion recipe on page 44.

Harvesting Tomatoes

As soon as the tomatoes have ripened to their full color, they are ready to pick. Tomatoes are one of our top five favorites to grow, as my children love to pick the fruits off the plants and pop them straight into their mouths. You can't beat a sun-ripened, homegrown tomato for a burst of delicious, juicy goodness. Pick off the individual ripe tomatoes as they are ready and leave the branches intact to continue growing the rest of the crop. If you end up with a glut of green tomatoes at the end of the season, with no sunshine left to ripen them, you have a couple of options for still using them. One is to place them all in a bowl or paper bag along with a ripe banana, which should give off chemicals that cause the tomatoes to get a hurry on and ripen themselves. Alternatively, there are great green-tomato chutney recipes you could try.

GROWING SUNFLOWERS

Sunflowers are a magnificent plant to grow in your garden. They're easy to grow, statuesque, and beautiful, and as they are loved by bees, they are very beneficial too. They are an excellent choice if you want your children to experience a full cycle of starting something from seed, seeing it grow almost in front of their eyes, and harvesting their own sustainable seeds for planting the following year.

Planting Sunflowers

You can grow tall or dwarf sunflowers, in shades from bright yellow through to dark purple and brown; but for a children's garden I would focus on the magic of growing something extremely tall that will tower over everyone's head and choose a variety such as Russian Giant, which can grow as high as ten feet. Sunflowers are hardy annuals, which means they can be grown outside in early spring, even before the frosts have finished, and will grow, flower, and produce seeds all within a one-year cycle.

Start your seeds off in early spring. You can plant the seeds out in your garden where you want the sunflowers to grow, but then you are at the mercy of slugs and snails, which can easily chomp their way through every new stem, leaving you with no sunflowers at all. We choose, from bitter experience, to start all of our sunflowers in pots and then plant them out in the garden once they are stronger, more established plants, around eight inches tall. Follow the Planting Seeds guide in the next section to get things started.

Nurturing Sunflowers

Sunflowers aren't called sunflowers without good reason, and your plants really will do best if you place them in a sunny location. It's best to grow sunflowers in open soil rather than containers, as this will allow their roots to get a good, deep hold in the ground, and you won't run the risk of top-heavy flowers toppling over small containers. There's usually no need to stake your plants or offer any extra support, unless you have a particularly windblown plot. Sunflowers that are exposed to general weather conditions actually benefit from having to cope with being blown a little, and you'll find they develop stronger, thicker stems. You don't need to feed sunflowers, and if there's sufficient rain you don't need to supplement them with any extra water once they've been planted. Just let nature do her thing.

Harvesting Sunflowers

You can pick sunflowers to go in a vase, but I think they are best left out in the garden, providing majestic color and attracting lots of bees and butterflies. You can watch as they grow tall, peel open their flower heads, and then ripen and develop a full head of seeds toward the end of the season. These seed heads are a rich source of food for birds, so leave some out over the winter for them to feed on. You can also harvest some of the seeds to plant again next year or to give away in exchange for donations for your garden plot. You'll find more ideas on harvesting your own seeds later in the book.

GROWING NASTURTIUMS

Nasturtium flowers are as beautiful as sunflowers, in a completely different way, giving children an interesting contrast. Much smaller than sunflowers, they creep and spread through your flower beds, up trellises, and over containers. Like sunflowers, they are loved by bees and butterflies and come in a variety of colors, from yellow through orange to reds and purples. They have lovely lily pad–like leaves, where butterflies often like to lay their eggs, and a peppery scent and taste. Both the flowers and the leaves are edible, adding a great pop of color and taste to salads.

Planting Nasturtiums

Nasturtiums are half-hardy annuals. This means they can be started from seed in greenhouses or indoors in spring but cannot be planted out in the garden until the risk of frosts has passed. Once outdoors, though, they provide a full summer of colorful flowers right through until the first frosts of autumn arrive. You can use the Planting Seeds guide in the next section to get your seeds off to a good start by planting them either directly in the soil in the garden or in pots or containers, or you can let them tumble downward from hanging baskets.

Nurturing Nasturtiums

If you are growing nasturtiums in containers, you'll need to make sure they are watered. They will crawl along the ground happily, or you might like to provide support, such as poles, arches, or a trellis, for them to climb up. If you remove flowers as they start to fade and make sure no seedpods develop, they will keep flowering for months.

Harvesting Nasturtiums

You can pick off leaves and flowers to add to salads throughout the summer. Choose smaller, newer leaves for a peppery rather than bitter taste. Nasturtiums are quite likely to seed themselves around the garden, and you'll spot new plants peeping up the following year. You can also collect the seeds, allow them to dry out, and then plant them the following spring. Your children might like to set up a seed swap and trade different colors and varieties with friends and neighbors.

GROWING LETTUCE

As a contrast to the potatoes and tomatoes, the final plant in my top five is one you can pick, eat, pick, eat, repeatedly, as the plant grows more throughout the summer—a cut-and-come-again lettuce.

Planting Lettuce

Some lettuces are varieties that produce a head of leaves that you pick all in one go and then the plant is finished, but there are other varieties that produce a crop of loose leaves that you can harvest, and then the plant will go on to grow two, three, or four more crops of leaves, which you can continue to pick and eat over time. These cut-and-come-again types, such as Salad Bowl and Bijou, do really well in containers, and they are a good choice for children who enjoy regularly being able to go and pick something to eat. They also germinate and grow quickly, meaning you could be eating homegrown food in just three or four weeks' time.

To plant lettuce, fill a small container with compost or rake over a patch of soil in the garden. Water the soil well, scatter the seeds, and then cover them with a gentle layer of compost. Watering before you place the seeds prevents them from being washed away or from all ending up in the same corner of your pot.

Nurturing Lettuce

Water your lettuce every few days. Check for slugs and snails and remove any you spot before they munch away your crop. A layer of coffee grounds around each plant is said to deter them.

Harvesting Lettuce

Regularly pick the leaves throughout the growing season to encourage more fresh growth. Lettuces are said to be soporific, as the milky sap within the leaves is thought to calm nerves and send you to sleep. You could try a lettuce sandwich for dinner to see if it gives your children a particularly good night's sleep.

A WORD ABOUT BEES

It's been estimated that one-third of all of our food supply relies on bees and the role they play in pollinating plants. Whether they're gathering nectar or specifically gathering pollen, they are essential for allowing plants to develop fruits and vegetables. Even self- and wind-pollinated plants do better when bees are also involved in pollination. They are vitally important to crops around the world and to the plants you are trying to grow in your own backyard.

Bees, however, are under threat, and their numbers are declining—whether due to the use of pesticides, monoculture farming, change of land use, or climate change. You have an opportunity in your own garden classroom to improve this situation by making your space bee friendly.

The good news is, what's good for bees is also a blessing for your garden. Avoid using pesticides and grow the type of flowers bees love. Their favorites seem to be native flowers with single blooms in open, daisy-like or long tubular shapes. These flowers are, of course, ever so pretty and thus make a lovely choice to include in your garden. You can plant a selection in flower beds, in containers, or right in among your fruit and vegetables. Try to include some of the following plants in your garden, for the benefit of all.

TEN GREAT PLANTS FOR BEES

Sunflowers	Marigolds
Comfrey	Red clover
Nasturtiums	Buddleia
Lavender	Honeysuckle
Cosmos	Verbena

— PLANTING SEEDS —

WHILE IT'S PERFECTLY FINE TO START your garden with plants from the nursery, growing plants from seeds gives children a look at the whole growing process, which is a complete hands-on science lesson, and teaches much about sustainability.

The basic essentials for planting a seed are pretty much the same whatever you are growing. Check the seed packet for any specific instructions and then use the following steps to get your garden started.

Take care opening your seed packets, as overenthusiastic young gardeners can cause them to go everywhere. It's a good idea to open the packets over a bowl. Take a little time to look closely at the seeds, perhaps making use of a magnifying glass. You'll notice there is a huge variety of shape, color, texture, and markings from one seed variety to another.

Gather everything you need so you have all of your equipment ready before you begin to plant. You'll need your seeds, pots or other containers, compost, trowel, and a can of water. It's likely some of your compost will be spilled as you plant, so whether you are indoors or out, it's a good idea to place a drop cloth under the area where you're working. This will catch the fallen compost and make it easy for you to gather it to be reused. I'd also recommend keeping the watering cans in a designated area just so you can keep control and avoid unnecessary spillages.

The planting of your seeds is the creation of your garden, and there is a huge benefit in including children in this stage of the process. They will feel a valuable sense of ownership of the plants that are grown and will also appreciate the whole cycle of the life of the plant. They will see science in action and understand the fundamental connection that plants have to the seasons, giving them so much more profound learning, as they have had hands-on involvement in this stage of the creation. They'll also enjoy the tremendous feeling of pride when they are able to harvest from the plants they helped to start. Little beats the joy of eating a ripe, juicy tomato that you planted yourself.

CHOOSE A CONTAINER

So many things can be used as a container to plant your seeds, and you can recycle lots of items you have around your home. You could use plastic, cardboard, or fiber plant pots bought from a nursery; tin cans; toilet-roll tubes; egg cartons or even eggshells; newspaper rolled into tubes; or you could even plant the seeds right in the ground.

Go on a scavenger hunt around the house and garden and see what you can find. Take care to choose containers with no sharp edges and make sure you add some drainage holes in the bottom so the young plants don't get waterlogged. Some plant pots, such as toilet-roll tubes and egg cartons, will allow strong roots to grow through them and will also degrade in the soil, so you don't even need to take the seedling out—just plant the whole pot straight in the soil.

FILL WITH SOIL

Use a good-quality, peat-free potting compost to give your seeds the best start.

ADD SOME WATER

Water the compost before you plant your seeds. This prepares the ground and encourages root growth down into the soil. It will also prevent the seeds from being washed away or out of place in a flood of eager watering.

PLANT YOUR SEEDS

Check the individual instructions on the packet for information about the particular plant you're growing to see how deep to plant the seeds and any other special growing details. As a general rule, the bigger the seeds, the deeper you plant them. Plant larger seeds farther apart to give them space to grow.

DON'T FORGET A LABEL

Make a label for your seeds so you can remember what you've planted, especially if you're planting several different varieties at once. (See Plant Labels on page 39 for ideas on making your own.)

PLANT POTS TO TRY

- Toilet-roll tubes with one end folded in to create the base
- Comics and newspapers rolled up into a pouch
- Tin cans
- Egg cartons
- Eggshells
- Yogurt pots
- Juice cartons
- Silicone cupcake cases
- The empty skin of half an avocado, orange, grapefruit, melon, pumpkin, or coconut shell
- Zipper plastic bags
- Storage boxes

EGG HEADS & TIN CAN HAIR SALON

THESE EGG HEADS AND TIN CAN people are a fun, first growing project for children to try. For both of these projects, the growing grass becomes the hair that can be clipped and styled. For the eggs, use markers and googly eyes to make faces. For the tin cans, use magnetic accessories to add faces.

MATERIALS

For the Egg Heads
- Empty eggshells (try to break off just the top to empty them so you have a good-size shell left to use)
- Empty egg carton
- Marker pens
- Stick-on googly eyes (optional but fun)
- Cotton balls
- Garden cress or grass seeds

For the Tin Can Hair Salon
- Empty tin (not aluminum) cans, lids removed with a can opener that leaves no sharp edges, and washed clean
- Card stock
- Scissors
- Pens and pencils
- Small magnets or magnetic strip
- Double-sided transparent tape or glue dots
- Compost
- Garden cress or grass seeds

Decide whether you'll be making egg heads or tin can people. If using eggs, wash out the eggshells and set them in the egg carton to keep them steady (place them on a cotton-ball cushion to raise them up a bit if you need to). If using cans, use a clean and empty tin can, with the lid removed with a can opener that leaves no sharp edges. Usually when we are planting anything, we make sure there are drainage holes at the base of the container. This time, as we're going to be playing with these egg heads and tin can people indoors and we don't want water running out over our play space, don't make any holes in the bottom. Do just take care not to overwater the plants.

Draw some crazy faces on your eggshells with markers, adding the googly eyes if you've got some. For the cans, use the card stock, pens, and pencils to draw some eyes, noses, mouths, glasses, bow ties, and hats. Cut out each item and attach a small magnet to the back with the double-sided transparent tape or glue dots. You could do self-portraits or funny faces.

Put some cotton balls inside the eggshells and dampen them with water. Sprinkle cress or grass seeds all over the cotton balls—good coverage will give you a full head of hair. Fill each tin can with compost, leaving about an inch free at the top. Sprinkle on some grass seeds and then cover the seeds with a little more compost. Place the eggshells or cans on a windowsill and wait for the hair to sprout. It'll take only a couple of days. Add a little bit of water if the cotton balls or compost dry out, but not too much.

Once your grass has grown a little, you're ready to set up your hair salon. You can add real hair clips and ponytail holders to the growing hair, and the great thing about using grass rather than cress for this project is that you can snip it into different styles and it will then grow back ready for another trim in a few days' time.

QUIRKY
── ECOPLANTERS ──

IT'S AMAZING JUST WHAT YOU CAN FIND to transform into a plant pot. Reuse and upcycle what you already have, are about to throw out, or can find in charity shops and create some quirky ecoplanters. Your garden is a children's space, and it's fun to include some unusual planters in the mix. The children will love them, and they'll catch the eye of people passing and make them smile.

Once you have seedlings sprouting from the potted seeds you have planted together, you need to think about preparing suitable homes for your growing plants to move into as they establish themselves. The potting compost you used with your seeds is great for the first few weeks of germination and growing, but the hungry plants will soon use up the nutrients within this starter compost. You can refer to your individual seed packets for specific timing on potting, but when your plants are a few weeks old and have their first few pairs of leaves, it's time to move them on to larger pots. This gives them more space to develop a strong root section and fill out and thrive. It will also allow you to relocate your plants to optimum locations around your garden classroom—in the sun or shade, both to suit the plant and to allow you to create a pretty garden design.

MATERIALS

- Planters (choose from the selection on the next page)
- Scissors, craft knife, and/or drill
- Compost
- Plants
- Cable ties and ribbon

Make sure every planter you are using has drainage holes in the bottom. Scissors or a craft knife does the job well in most of the containers, but you might need to use a drill for some of the metal items.

Fill each planter with good compost and then add your plants. Choose small plants such as pansies, trailing plants such as nasturtiums, or spring- and summer-flowering bulbs. Herbs and salad plants can grow well in the planters too. Use cable ties to fasten the planters to a fence, with some ribbon here and there to add extra color. Or line your planters in a row for a burst of splashy color.

ITEMS TO USE FOR PLANTERS

- Wellingtons or other rain boots
- Sneakers
- Tin cans
- Colanders
- Bread bins
- Clogs
- Teapots
- Plastic bottles
- Saucepans

- Buckets
- Pocket shoe organizers
- Fabric shopping bags
- Burlap sacks
- Tires
- Wine barrels
- Wheelbarrows
- Woolen socks
- Even a bathtub

PAINTED
PLANT POTS

THESE PAINTED PLANT POTS are a fun way to add some extra color to your garden. They're also perfect to give as gifts for birthdays or Mother's Day, especially with a homegrown plant inside.

MATERIALS

- Plant pot
- Wooden skewer and egg carton
- Pencil
- Acrylic paint
- Paintbrushes or cotton swabs
- White, or craft, glue

First, a clever way to hold the plant pot in place while you decorate it is to poke a wooden skewer into an egg carton, then set the plant pot on top, poking the skewer through the pot's drainage hole. The pot is held in place but can still rotate, so the children can decorate all the way around.

Draw on your design using a pencil to begin with—and anything goes: flowers, spots, stripes, a word, a name, a pattern. Then use acrylic paint to add color. Use fine paintbrushes, cotton swabs, or fingers to apply the paint.

To finish, brush a layer of watered-down white, or craft, glue over the painted pot when it is completely dry to help preserve the design.

GROW YOUR
— OWN MEADOW —

EVEN IF YOU HAVE a small urban garden, there's no reason that you can't grow your own meadow. A movable patch of lawn creates a beautiful play space for your children—inside or out. It also makes for an easy-to-grow first foray into gardening. It allows you to bring a little of the garden indoors, introducing a touch of nature to an inside play space, and it makes a fun, sensory base for imaginary play.

MATERIALS

- Seed tray
- Compost
- Grass seeds

Take a seed tray that is big enough to be a good play space for your children but small enough to move around easily (our seed tray was about 17¾ by 12 inches in size). Fill it with compost and water the soil.

Measure out some grass seeds (according to the seed-packet instructions) and sprinkle them over the compost, casting them in both horizontal and vertical lines to ensure good coverage.

Place your seed tray in a safe spot either indoors or outdoors and leave it, watering from time to time, until the seeds germinate. Within a week or two your meadow should begin to grow—and grow and grow and grow until you have a beautiful, verdant meadow, ready for play. Is it a farm, a jungle, a fairyland, or a dinosaur world? Move it inside and you have a natural, sensory play scene, bringing the beauty of the outdoors right inside your home. And when your meadow grows so much it needs a haircut, use a pair of scissors to give the lawn a trim.

—SNIPPING GARDEN—

EVERYONE LOVES PICKING FLOWERS and harvesting food from a garden, and including leaves and petals in play is a wonderful way to add additional sensory dimensions to everything children are doing in the garden. Of course, some plants are precious; fruits and vegetables need to remain on plants to give them time to mature or ripen, and we all like to enjoy flowers out in the garden rather than picking everything as soon as it appears. Setting up a snipping garden is the answer, as it creates a constant supply of goodies for the children to pick to use in play, while keeping other plants out of bounds, to be enjoyed in the garden or left until it's really time to harvest them.

MATERIALS

- Small container: you could use a plant pot, a bucket, or an area of the flower bed
- Compost
- Watering cans
- Selection of seeds or plants (see suggestions below)

Plant your snipping garden in a dedicated bed or in containers. If using a container, make sure there are drainage holes in the base and fill it with compost. Then add a selection of plants that the children can enjoy snipping to include in their play. Herbs and pretty flowers are great choices, offering color and scent. Good choices would be mint, basil, rosemary, lavender, cosmos, marigolds, wallflowers, and pansies.

-

PLANT LABELS

I FIND CHILDREN WHO are reluctant writers often turn out to be quite happy to pick up a pen and make their mark if the purpose of their writing is clear and they feel involved in a real, practical project. One such way to weave some reading and writing into your everyday gardening is to make your own plant labels.

At the beginning of the year, you'll need to create lots of plant labels so you can keep track of what is growing where in the garden. Set up a label-creation station, and the children can make colorful and useful signs for around the plot. Offer a selection of these materials, and everyone can pick a few of their favorites to create with.

CRAFT-STICK PLANT LABELS

Take some craft sticks and use permanent markers to write plant names on them. Add an illustration of each plant for added color. Paint the sticks with a layer of clear varnish to weatherproof your design.

PEBBLE PLANT LABELS

Use acrylic paints to draw and write on flat pebbles, again using a coat of varnish afterward to protect the illustration.

PAPER PLANT LABELS

You can also use paper or card stock to create an easy set of plant labels, particularly for indoor plants. Putting each plant label through a laminating machine can help protect it and give it a measure of weatherproofing. Cut out flower shapes or rectangles, add your words and pictures, and fasten the label to a twig or a wooden skewer.

CLOTHESPIN PLANT LABELS

Use a permanent marker to draw and write your plant information on a clothespin; you'll find they are supereasy to clamp onto a stick in your plant pots.

CHALKBOARD PLANT LABELS

A chalkboard technique is useful for making a set of plant labels you can use over and over again. Apply chalkboard paint to your choice of plant label, whether it's a pebble, twig, craft stick, or clothespin. These are useful in the spring when you're growing lots of seeds in succession. You can write the name of your plant on your labels as you sow the seeds; then when you have grown the seedlings and planted them out, you can wipe the wording off each chalkboard label and use it again for your next batch of seeds.

WOODEN-SPOON PLANT LABELS

Wooden spoons make great plant markers too. Use markers or paints to add your plants' names, and cover them with a protective layer of varnish before you place the labels out in the garden.

—DIY WATERING CAN—

CHILDREN LOVE TO WATER PLANTS. Generally this is
good news, and watering is a helpful chore the children can take on
in the garden. Sometimes, though, overenthusiastic watering can be
bad news—plants can become waterlogged and seedlings can rot away.
Sometimes seedlings can be damaged in a deluge, and sometimes, especially in a class garden, you simply don't have enough watering cans
to go around. This DIY watering can with a rose head could be the ideal
solution. Made from a plastic milk bottle or similar carton, it's free and
a great way to upcycle your junk into something practical. It's easy to
make and holds just the right amount of water, so it's not too heavy
for young children, and everyone can take a turn at watering without
causing a flood.

MATERIALS

- 1-quart plastic milk or juice bottle with a lid
- Craft knife or scissors

Start by washing out your milk bottle. We use a quart-size bottle, which gives enough room to fill with a good amount of water without the bottle's being too heavy.

Use a knife or a pair of scissors to make small holes in the bottle's lid. Give the knife a little wiggle to create a hole rather than a slit, to allow the water to come out freely. Always consider safety: this might be a job for an adult.

Remove the bottle top to fill your new watering can with water, pop the lid back on, and you're ready to go. The handle on the bottle makes it comfortable to hold, and if necessary, a gentle squeeze can help the water come out.

GARDEN
— POWER POTION —

ALL THE TIME WE'RE PLAYING and learning in our garden classroom, we're working alongside nature. Perhaps the most important lesson children are absorbing is that they are part of something bigger. Although they might make the choice to grow certain plants, they can't do it alone. They need the natural forces of soil and air and water to help. Sometimes being part of this community of plants and animals works against us, and aphids, for example, arrive to suck the juice from our freshly planted flowers. Sometimes, though, we can harness the natural forces of the garden and use them to our advantage. Here's one way: make a garden power potion.

MATERIALS

- Large container, such as a bucket, with a lid
- Leaves from comfrey, dandelions, nettles, and/or dock
- Gloves
- Water

A garden power potion harnesses the vital nutrients held within the soil and plants and lets you release them, to the benefit of your crops. We're going to make our own garden fertilizer from plants that might otherwise be considered weeds.

First, prepare your potion container. You'll need a large bucket or similar container that has a lid. The potion needs to be left to brew for some time, and the lid will help to prevent spills and keep any creatures from finding their way into the water; it will also contain the aroma of the potion, as things are going to get rather smelly.

Never miss the opportunity to add some writing in your classroom. The children can design a label for their garden-power-potion pot.

Then go foraging around your garden or out and about. You need to collect the leaves from comfrey, dock, nettles, or dandelions. You can stick with just one type of leaf (comfrey being my favorite for the job) or make a cocktail. You might like to set aside a patch of your garden specifically for growing a crop of these plants so you can sustain the production of your garden power potion from year to year. The fertilizer you'll produce is so good it's worth taking the time and space to make.

Comfrey, dock, nettle, and dandelion have been used to produce fertilizers for centuries, and the plants themselves are also beneficial, as they will attract pollinating bees and butterflies to your garden. They have deep roots that extract nutrients from within the soil. Nettles can sting, of course, so be sure to wear suitably protective gloves when picking them—or just leave them out of the mix altogether.

Gather enough leaves to fill your bucket and then pour in water to cover the plants. Fasten the lid on and leave your power potion to brew. Give it an occasional stir with a long stick if you like, and say a wish or a prayer of thanks to nature for providing you with rich food.

Some gardeners like to leave the potion for a whole year, by which time the smell should have dissipated, making the liquid fertilizer more pleasant to use, but it will be ready to use as early as eight weeks after you prepare it—albeit with a rather pungent aroma. Strain off the liquid into a bottle ready for use, and add the spent plant leaves to your compost heap.

To use the garden power potion to feed your plants, dilute one measure of the liquid with ten measures of water. Then use it to water your plants. It's packed full of potassium and is extremely beneficial to flower and fruit-producing plants.

HARVESTING YOUR
—— OWN SEEDS ——

AS YOU REACH THE END of your growing year, one lovely
activity to try with your children is to harvest the seeds from your own
plants. Gathering the seeds from things you planted yourself completes
the circle of the year and shows children how nature continues from
one year to the next. It lets you explore ideas of sustainability and self-
sufficiency and gently touches on ideas of life, death, and renewal, which
you might choose to relate to your own religious or spiritual beliefs. It's
quite a magical moment the following spring, when you see new shoots
appearing from seeds you've harvested from your own garden.

The seeds you collect are also great for swapping or fund-raising, which will enable you to obtain new materials for your garden. One single sunflower head alone will produce hundreds of seeds. Package these up and swap them with friends, neighbors, and other schools, giving them your seeds and getting different varieties back from them in exchange. You might also like to sell packets of seeds to parents and other supporters, raising funds that you might donate to a favorite charity or use to buy new equipment for your garden classroom.

HOW TO COLLECT YOUR OWN SEEDS

A dry, early fall day is the best time to gather seeds. Your aim is to harvest a variety of seeds from around your garden and to store them over the winter. You'll want to label them carefully so you know exactly what you are planting when you begin the garden again next year.

SUNFLOWERS

Once the flower petals have faded on your sunflowers, allow the seed heads to dry out for a while—you can cut them and hang them in a porch or leave them on their stems in the garden if the weather is dry, although you may find some seeds are eaten by birds. Then gently rub off the papery top layer of the seed heads and use your thumbs to brush out all the seeds into a container. You could get thousands from one garden alone. Sunflower seeds are a good source of food for birds over the winter, so you might like to leave one of the full seed heads out in the garden for them.

POPPIES AND NICOTIANA

If you have poppies or nicotiana in the garden, go and give their seed heads a gentle shake and you'll hear all the seeds inside. Put a plastic or paper bag over the seed head, carefully turn it upside down, and shake out all the seeds before they're dispersed across the garden in the wind.

NASTURTIUMS

Toward the end of the summer, look at the soil underneath where your nasturtiums have been growing and you will find the plants' seedpods, which may be green, or brown if they've already begun to dry. Leave them to germinate where they are, ready for next year, or gather them up, place them in a paper bag to dry out until spring, and then use them to plant, swap, or sell.

MAKE SEED PACKETS FOR YOUR SEED SWAPS

To package seeds, you can buy little glassine packets, often used by stamp collectors, which make perfect seed packets, or you can use small envelopes. I would avoid using plastic bags, because they may retain moisture and the seeds could become damp and spoil. Fill each packet with a number of your seeds, keeping each variety separate to avoid any surprises when they grow. Take some sheets of sticky labels and have the children draw pictures on them and write the names of the plants the seeds have come from. Peel off the labels and place one on each packet of seeds, which will give you a decorative set of seed packets to share.

—— GETTING FREE STRAWBERRY PLANTS ——

If you have access to a strawberry patch, look for strawberry plants sending out runners in the later summer and autumn. Each plant will grow long white stems, and you will notice a set of leaves appearing at the end of each one. Place a plant pot full of compost underneath this baby set of leaves, and the plant will send down roots into the soil in your plant pot. Once it's gotten a hold in the soil, you can cut this baby plant free from the runner stem, giving you a new plant to grow and then plant in your garden, providing lots more strawberries for free next year.

PLAY &
IMAGINATION

CHILDREN LEARN BEST through play. It's fundamentally in their nature and gives them opportunities to develop skills, try out new ideas, and make connections in their learning. While you are planning projects for science, math, and literacy for your garden classroom, also be sure to schedule time, create space, and provide encouragement for play.

In this chapter you will find activity suggestions for fun times and also ideas you can use to make play spaces in your garden that your children can use all year-round. You'll find ideas for equipping your garden to encourage den building and creative play with loose parts. There are fairy and dinosaur worlds for imaginary play, and tea party and pretend play potting-shed ideas for role-playing. And there are also suggestions for sensory play for each season of the year.

LOOSE-PARTS PLAY

The term *loose parts* simply means movable materials that children can use in their play. They might be materials you've bought or upcycled from the recycling bin, or they could be found natural objects. The garden, a park, or a woodland can be a rich source of free, natural loose parts that are a valuable inclusion for play and learning in your garden classroom. A garden classroom well stocked with loose parts offers children daily inspiration, endless possibilities, a chance to think, and encouragement to be creative.

We're talking about creative play not only from an artistic point of view—although loose parts do provide great materials with which to sculpt and build—but also as play that encourages brain development, scientific experimenting, mathematical thought, risk taking, and trial and error learning.

Through this kind of free play, children are really creating: using what they have and what they already know and combining that to create a whole that's greater than the parts, just like Einstein, da Vinci, and Steve Jobs. Loose parts and free play in childhood develop the creative genius of the future. To promote this kind of creative learning, consider the following suggestions:

- Have loose parts in your garden classroom all the time so the children get familiar with what's available and can include them in their play when they get an idea.
- Add new materials from time to time to spark fresh thinking. Particularly in a garden classroom, it is good to change some of the items available to match the seasons of the year. You can use the list on page 56 for some suggestions.
- Make sure the children have lots and lots of time to investigate, explore, daydream, and make use of the loose parts. This book is full of ideas you can use for activities and lessons, but it is just as important to schedule time for free play in your garden classroom, where the children can enjoy the environment without any structured activities.
- Have other children and adults available to help problem solve, to add twists to the play, and to admire creations and inventions. Let the children lead in the fort building and small-world creating, but be there to assist when needed.

You don't need to think about how the children might use the materials—leave that to the kids. Provide the loose parts, step back, and let the children play. They might surprise you with their imaginations and create things you would never have dreamed up.

IDEAS FOR MATERIALS
FOR YOUR PLAY SPACE

The great thing about stocking your play space with loose parts is that anything goes (so long as the materials are suitable for your children's ages and stages) and they're mainly free. Collecting natural materials; recycled items; and donations from friends, family, and local businesses are all great ways to get your loose parts. And your garden itself can be a rich source of loose parts. Here are some items you might like to include:

- Leaves
- Rocks and pebbles
- Shells
- Twigs and branches
- Seedpods and large seeds
- Wood scraps
- Planks of wood
- Slices of wood from tree trunks
- Flowers
- Moss
- Guttering pipes and connectors
- Flowerpots
- Yarn and string
- Ribbon
- Pots and pans
- Funnels

- Squirt bottles
- Nuts and bolts
- Slate tiles
- Buckets
- Feathers
- Cupcake liners
- Cookie cutters
- Pinecones
- Flags
- Potato mashers
- Pens and pencils
- Clipboards
- Garden poles (beanpoles)
- Pieces of fabric
- Clothespins

HOW TO
— BUILD A FORT —

FORTS OPEN UP A WORLD OF IMAGINARY play for children, developing creativity, design, problem solving, and construction skills all at the same time. Most children don't need to be shown how to build a fort—it seems to come naturally—but making sure they have plenty of suitable materials available can really encourage this kind of play. You may have a permanent playhouse structure, but offering lots of loose parts enables children to work together to build a fort from their imagination. The garden offers a prime spot for fort building, as there is space to construct and often natural materials readily available with which to build. There is also something elemental about building a fort outdoors—claiming your own patch of the world and setting up home.

ESSENTIAL INGREDIENTS FOR FORTS

There are no strict rules about building a fort—other than having consideration for safety—and the fort can be as simple or as elaborate as your children wish. However, a little thought concerning the essential ingredients for forts can help children get the most from the experience.

SPACE

Children can build a den anywhere: under a tree, with fabric over a clothesline, in a shady corner of the garden, or in a forest. Let your children have some freedom to choose the location of their den, perhaps agreeing together on some safety and practical arrangements first. How long will the construction be allowed to remain, and will they agree to help tidy it away afterward?

MATERIALS

Great building materials include big branches, garden umbrellas laid on their side, garden chairs and tables, cushions and blankets, bed sheets and big pieces of fabric, and crates and boxes. Scarves, string, and clothespins are useful for fastening things together. Oversize cardboard boxes make instant forts.

PROPS

The addition of the right props can transform a den into a whole day's worth of happy play. Have dedicated outdoor items readily available or encourage the children to bring things from indoors out into the garden. Props that spark great play include pots and pans and picnic items, flashlights, pillows, and sleeping bags or blankets. Children will often camp out in a den and read and draw, so have a basket of books, clipboards, and pencils ready for them to use.

PRETEND-PLAY
— POTTING SHED —

TO GET ALL THE BENEFITS gardening offers, it's good to let children be as hands-on as possible. Of course, some seeds are precious, and new plants are delicate, and that's not always the best combination with a young child who wants to plant and pick and poke. A solution for keeping everyone happy is to set up a potting-shed play area where the kids can role-play being gardeners over and over again to their hearts' content—giving the real plants in the garden a chance to get established while the children are playing elsewhere.

MATERIALS

- Plant pots and seed trays
- Small trowels and spades
- Compost, sand, rice, dried pasta, or playdough
- Seeds and artificial flowers
- Watering cans, spray bottles
- Seed packets and garden catalogs
- Plant labels
- Pencils, paper, and clipboards or chalkboards and chalk

Choose an area in the garden where your kids can putter and make a little mess. A shady spot under a canopy or tree is ideal, as the children can play as long as they like and still be sheltered from the sun.

Gather some materials to equip your planting station. A raised sandbox makes a great potting table. Add plant pots, seed trays, and small trowels and spades.

You'll need planting material, but what you choose is up to you and how much mess you enjoy. Compost is the obvious choice, but sand, rice, dried pasta, and even playdough are all good options for filling plant pots to plant seeds and flowers in.

Provide things for your children to plant. You could offer spare seeds, especially big ones such as beans, peas, or sunflowers, which children can handle easily and reuse each time they play.

Add artificial flowers, too, either bought or homemade. (The Spring Flower Bouquet craft on page 168 offers some ideas for flowers you could make.)

Include watering cans and spray bottles to tend the plants, filled with water or just imagination.

Never miss an opportunity to add reading, writing, and math. Provide some real seed packets and pages from garden catalogs to browse through, covering them with contact paper or sticky-back plastic or laminating them if you want to help them last longer outdoors. Keep a supply of plant labels and pencils so the children can write notes about what they've planted. Clipboards with paper or a chalkboard are good ways to provide writing surfaces outside, and the children can chart what they've planted or even set up a nursery and sell their wares.

MUD-PIE
TEA PARTY

GLORIOUS MUD! It's the essential fine-dining ingredient in a mud-pie kitchen. Hosting an afternoon tea party in your garden offers lots of opportunity for sensory play, teamwork, language development, reading, writing, counting, and wonderful imaginary play.

MATERIALS

- Range of sensory materials such as mud, water, sand, leaves, flowers and petals, herbs, and berries
- Selection of pots, pans, plates, teacups, and teapots
- Cookie cutters and cupcake liners
- Doilies and cake stands
- Picnic blanket or table and chairs
- Bunting, if you really want to set the scene
- Friends or toys to join in the banquet

What delights could you serve your guests at an afternoon tea party in your garden? Mud cakes, flower cookies, dainty sandwiches made from leaves. With a role-play activity such as this one, I like to think of the adults as facilitators rather than direct participants. Our role is to offer the materials as an invitation to play and then to step back and let the children take over. Give them space and time to imagine and create. Yes, accept cups of tea and slices of mud cake if offered, but be mindful of letting the children own the game and take the lead in the way it develops. As they play, you'll notice the games are full of learning.

- They'll try out new language and develop conversation skills as they chat, take orders, request ingredients, and serve guests.
- Notice how math weaves into the play as they make sure every person has a teacup, as they count out cookies onto a plate, as they match up the right-colored cups with saucers.
- Observe how they work on fine-motor skills as they pick leaves and petals to decorate their cakes or write down the menu on a chalkboard.
- They're also working with science as they concoct food from mud, sand, and water, experimenting with different substances and learning how materials combine and change states.
- They also get to develop relationships with others, enjoying fun times together and working as a team to organize the party and take on different roles in the play.

FAIRY GARDEN

EVERY OUTDOOR PLAY SPACE can benefit from the addition of an imaginary play space. Playing in a "small world" stretches children's imaginations away from everyday situations and encourages them to think creatively. Combining natural materials lets them enjoy many different textures and colors and work out inventive ways to use them. It helps children's language skills, too, as they think up characters and conversations.

MATERIALS

- Patch of ground or a container filled with soil
- Grass seed or moss
- Gravel and pebbles
- Plant pot or fairy house
- Small plants and flowers
- Loose parts collected from the garden: shells, bark, twigs, and string

Start by choosing a location for your fairy garden. There are many possibilities: a patch of soil, a plant pot, half of a water barrel, an old wheelbarrow, an old suitcase, a wooden treasure chest, a large plastic box. Make a few drainage holes in the base of the container.

Next fill your container with soil and then create your magical land. You might like to sow some grass seeds or cover the surface with moss. Gravel and tiny pebbles make good pathways. Find somewhere for your fairies to live: an old plant pot is perfect. Add some trees and flowers. You might like to transfer some from elsewhere in the garden or sow some wildflower seeds. Shells can be used for sidewalks or decorative edging. Bark makes a good fairy seat. Twigs can be pushed into the soil, with twine woven through to make fences. Or bind some sticks at the top to make a tent or archway.

You can make fairies from clothespins with doily wings and invite them to come and live in your garden.

MAKE A
—DINOSAUR WORLD—

ISN'T IT AMAZING to think that once it was dinosaurs rather than bugs and beetles that roamed in your garden? With a few props and

some imagination, you can create your own miniature dinosaur world in your garden classroom for all sorts of imaginary play. Many children seem to have a natural curiosity about dinosaurs; and especially if a fairy garden isn't their thing, dinosaurs can be just right as a stepping-stone into pretend play in the garden.

MATERIALS

- Patch of ground or a container filled with soil
- Rocks
- Grasses and other plants
- Toy dinosaurs

Begin by selecting a container: a big plant pot, a plastic storage box, or an old suitcase. It's good to choose a container that's big enough for a few children to play with together. Try to find something that is accessible from all sides of the area or even big enough to sit in while playing. Make a few drainage holes in the base and then fill it with soil. Add a few rocks of different shapes and sizes to give the dinosaurs an interesting habitat. Include plants for the dinosaurs to eat and hide among. Grasses work well, as they are fairly robust and can stand up to some play and can be trimmed when they start to get overgrown. A saucer or plant-pot base full of water can make a swamp. Then it's up to the children to play.

Small-world play, in setups like this dinosaur world, really encourages children to stretch their imagination and develop language skills. If you sit alongside and listen and observe how they play, you'll see how the children tell stories and cooperate with others. And of course the dinosaur world makes an excellent springboard into a prehistory project.

MINIATURE
GARDEN

A MINIATURE GARDEN makes a wonderful child-size space for some small-world play. This miniature garden can be a dream garden for little people to live in. It's like a dollhouse for the outdoors and a space in which to imagine and tell stories. Unlike a real garden, in this miniature world you can make dramatic design changes instantly—and at little or no cost. For children who love crafts and making things, this is a space they can come back to time and time again, adding new features and changing the design. You can also use the miniature garden to focus on the changes of season: revisit your space throughout the year and modify it to reflect how your real garden looks at different times of the year.

MATERIALS

- Container filled with soil
- Twigs, craft sticks, string
- Gravel, shells, pebbles
- Food jar lids, tin foil, small mirrors
- Small plants, moss, bark
- Dollhouse furniture

To make a miniature garden of your own, first choose a container: an ice-cream tub, a big plant pot, or an under-bed storage box works well. Then prepare the ground. If you're going to grow real plants in your miniature garden, make some drainage holes in the bottom of your container, then fill it with soil. You can still bring your miniature garden inside to play with—just set it on a tray to catch any drips.

Use craft sticks and twigs to build fencing and make tepees for your plants to grow on. Gravel and shells can be used for paths. Lids from food jars, tinfoil, or small mirrors can create a pond. Select plants that will stand up to some play and will retain a miniature size. We like using grasses, which are fun to give a haircut, and easy-maintenance plants such as hens and chicks (*Sempervivum*; also called houseleeks). For some prettiness you can add tiny violas.

Once your plants are in place, add some embellishments. Borrow items from your dollhouse to make a seating area, or make some chairs and a table using corks and pebbles. Use twigs or wooden kitchen skewers and string to make a clothesline or some bunting. Find seeds to place in rows to make a vegetable garden. Let the children use their imagination and see what they can create.

GARDEN
— SENSORY TUBS —

WE ALL LEARN through our senses, but perhaps especially in the early years when every color, scent, and texture is new. The garden abounds with things to look at, touch, and smell, but we're not always happy to let our children loose to pick anything and everything. A garden sensory tub lets us set up a minigarden for our children to explore that's filled with carefully chosen materials. We can use the tubs for play and also for math and literacy learning activities.

MATERIALS

- Container to hold your sensory materials—something large enough to hold a good variety of resources but small enough so your child can sit or stand alongside and easily be able to reach inside
- Base material that you can use to fill the tub and that can be changed to match each season: clean compost, grass cuttings, leaves, sand, water, or mud
- Selection of added extras to bring lots of sensory interest to your tub: Items from the garden can include flowers, leaves, pebbles, seed heads, pinecones, plant pots, trowels, and small spades. Items borrowed from indoors can include small toys such as animals and little people, pots, and scoops.

To make your sensory tub, fill your container with base material and then start to introduce the extras. Invite your children to explore the materials. Younger children are likely to enjoy simply exploring the sensory properties of the materials on offer: touching, scooping, pouring, spilling, gathering, and sprinkling. The tub is like a treasure chest as they hunt for the hidden gems buried inside. Older children can use the sensory tub as a spark for imaginary play, and they can use the available materials to create play scenes and pretend lands.

You can vary the contents of your sensory tub to match each season in your garden. In spring you can fill the tub with clean compost and add plant pots, trowels, large seeds, and pretend flowers for scooping and filling and pretending to plant. In summer you might use green leaves or grass cuttings as the base for your tub and add flowers and toy butterflies and bugs. In fall, autumn leaves provide a colorful and crunchy base. In winter you might like to swap things around and use the sensory tub to bring some of the garden indoors. If you have snow, scoop some into your tub and bring it inside to play with.

It's also possible to use these tubs for sensory learning that incorporates math and literacy. Whatever letters, shapes, numbers, or words you are working on can be hidden in the sensory tubs for your children to hunt for. Prepare some cards with sight words and hide them in the tub. See if they can fish them out and read the words out loud.

Hide fridge-magnet letters in the tub and see if they can use them to spell out some words. Have them use both hands to hunt for number cards and then see if they can add them together. Classify your children's finds and have them make piles of green leaves, red leaves, and yellow leaves.

Make sure the tubs and the scoops you provide with the tubs are in a variety of shapes and sizes so the children can explore volume and dimension as they play.

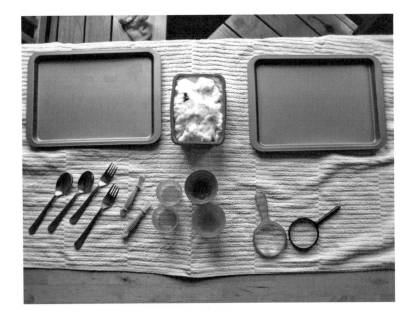

SENSORY
— TREASURE HUNT —

A GARDEN IS such a rich sensory playground for children to explore. This treasure-hunt activity encourages children to focus on the wide variety of scents, colors, and textures surrounding them.

MATERIALS

- Egg carton
- Pens or paints
- Fabric scraps

To prepare for your sensory treasure hunt, take an egg carton and use each section as a different sensory clue to matching objects the children will hunt for. You can make these clues yourself in advance or have the children create them. In a class, pairs of children could make a carton and then swap it with another pair for the hunt.

For seeing, paint some of the egg-carton sections in colors you can find in your garden. You might like to encourage the children to focus on the fine differences and include different shades of green for them to try to match exactly.

For touching, glue scraps of fabric into some of the egg-carton sections to give a range of textures for the children to feel. Could they find something in the garden that feels like silk, velvet, or sandpaper?

For smelling, add a few drops of an essential oil to one of the sections, or rub it with the crushed leaves of an herb. It's best to keep these scented clues at opposite ends of the egg carton to help keep each smell separate and easier to distinguish.

Once you've prepared your treasure cartons, head out into your garden classroom and see what you can find. The children could pick a little sample of each matching plant they find and bring the items back to show the group. You might like to race to see who can find all the matching treasures the fastest, or you might prefer to take your time and enjoy exploring with all the senses you can.

PLAYDOUGH IN THE GARDEN

ANYTHING THAT YOU ENJOY playing with inside can be taken outdoors, too, and playdough is no exception. It's a wonderful sensory material—so good for tactile play and building fine-motor skills and as a prompt for imaginary play—and it combines wonderfully with garden petals.

MATERIALS

- Playdough (see recipe on page 77)
- Loose parts collected from the garden: leaves, twigs, pebbles, berries, flower petals

There are many ways playdough can enhance your play and learning in the garden. Here are some ideas to get you started:

> Pick and chop some herb leaves and add them to the dough mix for an additional sensory element. Playdough with added rosemary, oregano, or thyme makes the perfect dough for pretend pizzas. Add seeds to the dough to provide an interesting texture.

> Pick some petals and use them to make patterns in your dough. For a sensory math lesson, try making circular mandala designs or other repeating patterns.

> Use some sticks from the garden to make marks in the dough, practicing shapes or letters.

> Use the dough as the base for imaginary lands, using loose parts such as leaves, pebbles, twigs, and berries to make buildings, paths, and other props for pretend play.

> Explore the shapes and structures of the plants in your garden by taking leaves and stems and using them to make prints in your playdough, noticing all the details that the plant parts imprint in the dough.

HOMEMADE PLAYDOUGH RECIPE

Making your own playdough is quick, easy, and inexpensive. It allows you to make large batches, giving the children plenty to play with, and lets you add lots of different colors, scents, and textures that you can't find in store-bought dough.

INGREDIENTS

- 2 cups flour
- 1 cup salt
- 2 tablespoons cream of tartar
- 2 tablespoons vegetable oil
- 1½ cups water just at the boiling point
- Food coloring (optional)
- Essential oils (optional)
- Chopped herbs (optional)
- Glitter (optional)

To make a batch of homemade playdough, simply mix all the ingredients together in a large bowl. You can add any extras you like at this stage: food coloring, essential oils for scents, chopped herbs, or glitter. Stir all the ingredients together and then knead the mixture for a minute or two to form a dough. Then you're ready to play.

SNAIL RACES

HOLDING A SNAIL RACE lets you have a good close-up look at these garden creatures. Remember to treat the snails responsibly and handle them very carefully.

MATERIALS

- Chalk
- Snails
- Stopwatch

Use chalk to draw your racetrack on a patio or sidewalk. You could try traditional lanes, but your snails might not race in a straight line. Alternatively, make a circular bull's-eye racecourse and start all the snails in the center. Whichever snail gets to the outside circumference first is the winner. You could set up a chart to record each snail's progress and use a stopwatch to time them.

Use the race as an opportunity to get a good look at the snails. Watch how they move and look around. See if all of their shells look exactly the same. You might like to sketch the winning snail and include your drawing in your garden journal.

READING & WRITING

AUTHORS, POETS, AND PLAYWRIGHTS have been inspired by the natural environment for centuries, and a garden classroom can be a spark to encourage our children's literacy too. As we will see later in the book with math and science, the very fact that you are gardening opens up opportunities to broaden your children's knowledge in areas of literacy. They will encounter new vocabularies such as the names for parts of a plant and concepts such as germination and pollination, annual and perennial plants, and evergreen and deciduous trees. They will read seed packets and planting instructions and write seed labels naturally, as part of their gardening. In addition, there are ways to more formally enhance the literacy work that takes place in your garden classroom.

In this chapter you will find ideas for promoting reading, storytelling, and writing—be it scientific reporting, journaling, or creative writing. We'll also look at how we can weave words into our play and outdoor activities.

READING AND WRITING IN THE GARDEN

Your garden classroom offers the opportunity to take your traditional classroom-based learning outdoors, to allow the children to develop their skills in active, hands-on ways. Here are some ways you can learn reading and writing skills outside. They offer a series of activities that include kinesthetic/physical, visual, spatial, and sensory learning, all of which suit many different learning styles and help children use all of their senses for deeper, more effective learning.

LEAF LETTERS

Transform some leaves into a set of letter manipulatives for play and learning in the garden. Simply use paint or markers to write on each leaf. Make an alphabet or a group of spelling words. As soon as your paint is dry, you're ready to play and learn. You can combine the letters in a sensory tub or play with them on the grass or

driveway. Try stringing up a clothesline and pinning up the leaf letters to make words. You can vary the games to suit the different ages and stages of your children.

STICK SPELLING

Collect some sticks from around the garden and keep them available in a basket for the children to use. The sticks make good pencils for writing letters and words in mud or the sandbox or to dip in water so you can write on the driveway. You can also use the sticks themselves to form letters and build words: lay out the sticks on the ground to make letter shapes.

CHALK ALPHABET SPLAT

Use chalk to write out a whole alphabet of letters on the floor or wall—or use paint to create a permanent set. Use these letters for some gross-motor play and literacy learning. If your alphabet is on the floor, the children can jump or hop from letter to letter. If your alphabet is on the wall, they can "splat," or slap, the letters with their hands or throw balls or beanbags at them. For some water play, they can shoot water pistols at the letters.

You can vary your splat activities to suit the level of the children:

- Shout out a letter and see if the children can find it and splat it (or jump on it).
- Ask "What does . . . begin with?"
- Ask "What's the last letter sound in the word . . . ?"
- Shout out a spelling word and see if they can jump or splat all the letters in it in the right order.

MAKE YOUR WORDS DISAPPEAR

Use chalk to write a series of words that the children are working on, either on the floor or on the wall. Give a child a bucket of water and a paintbrush. Then call out a word and see if the child can find it in the mix of words available. Let the child paint over each letter of the word with water, tracing the shape of the letters and making them disappear.

RAINBOW WORDS

Give your children a set of chalks in all the colors of the rainbow. Write down a letter or a word for them in chalk and then have them write over the top of each letter using their own chalks. Write over the word in red, then write over the word in orange, then write over it in yellow…layering the colors until you have a complete rainbow word. Using this rainbow technique lets them benefit from the repetition of the letters, following the flow of the word.

HOPSCOTCH WORDS

Draw a hopscotch board on the sidewalk or driveway with chalk and write a word in each square. Hop and jump your way along, reading and saying each word aloud as you land on it.

CHECKERBOARD READ AND SAY

Draw a checkerboard on the sidewalk or driveway using chalk, making each square big enough for a child to stand in. Write a word in each square, using vocabulary words that you are currently learning, and mark a start and a finish square. Then play a game where you have to jump your way around the checkerboard from start to finish. Change the rules to suit different learning objectives: hop only on words that begin with "b," hop only on words that rhyme, hop only on words that start with "ch"…Read and say aloud each word as you land on it.

You can have these literacy activities available in your garden classroom right through the year, adapting the words in use to reflect your children's development through reading, writing, and spelling. Let's also look at other projects we can use outdoors to enrich the literacy work in the garden.

Here are three quick and easy ways to bring reading and writing outdoors.

GO INSIDE OUT

Set up a writing station in the garden: a tub of pencils on a picnic table; a bucket of chalk on the patio; an easel in the shade of a tree; a roll of paper fastened against a wall. Pretty much any way you promote writing inside works outdoors too.

STORY TENT

As you'll be thinking of providing somewhere shady for the children to keep cool, why not transform your shelter into a story tent? Add some big cushions for lounging on and a pile of books. Choose some great outdoor-themed stories and include information books on plants and animals so your young scientists can read up on the nature they observe outside.

CLIPBOARDS

A practical way to promote literacy outside is to have a stash of clipboards and pencils piled up near the door of your story tent, ready for action. The clipboards provide a sturdy base for writing and are easily taken out and about in the garden, the woods, or wherever you're playing outside.

WRITE A
— GARDEN JOURNAL —

A GARDEN JOURNAL is a great way to bring literacy outside into your garden and give children the opportunity to write with a practical purpose. See pages 199–216 for sample garden-journal pages that you can use with your children.

A garden journal can be a collaborative project, with everyone adding notes and draw-ings, or the children can each create their own. Keeping your journal within easy reach, rather than stored away on a bookshelf, encourages children to add notes whenever they see something interesting outside. You can mix in photos, sketches, and writing so children of any age can contribute. Here are some items you can note in your garden journal:

- Diary entries of your progress—what you planted, when things began to grow, what you've been enjoying outside
- Photos and drawings of the plants and animals you observe
- Treasures such as seeds, dried leaves, seed packets, and labels stuck onto the pages
- Scientific and mathematical data showing how high plants are growing and what conditions they like

At the end of the growing year, you'll have created a beautiful record of all the fun you've had in the garden that year.

In addition to using your journal as a record of the things you have grown, you can use it as a spark for creative writing and drawing. Try these prompts to spark some interesting journal entries:

- Pick one plant and then draw sketches of it every week as it grows and changes.
- Try some word art. Draw a picture in the center of your journal page of something from your garden, then fill the whole of the rest of the page with words that de-scribe your picture or come to mind when you think of it.
- Sit for a few minutes in silence in your garden and then make a list of everything you can hear.
- Focus on your senses and complete the sentences: Today in the garden I can see . . . , I can smell . . . , I can touch . . . , I can hear . . . , I can taste . . .
- Jot down a to-do list of all the garden chores you want to complete this week.
- You might like to keep a tally of your total food harvest for the year.
- Try a quick word-association list. What's the first thing you think of when you hear the words *leaf, flower, bird, soil, rain, sunshine, growth, harvest, bee, butterfly*?

- Make a list of every creature that lives in your garden.
- Write down three ordinary things you saw in your garden today. Then write down three extraordinary things you saw too.
- Imagine a garden in another land and environment. Write down a description of this place.
- Write a garden snapshot on one particular day. What's the weather like today? What's growing well? What animals can you see? What's ready to pick? Try this again during another season and see how your snapshot is different.
- Write seven words to describe the garden today.
- Note down one thing in the garden you'd like to learn more about. Then add some notes once you've done some research.
- Note down five things you know about potatoes, about sunflowers, about rain, about butterflies....
- Gather some leaves and capture them in your journal. Sketch one, press one, laminate one, and take a crayon rubbing of one.
- Try out many different art materials to draw flowers, leaves, creatures, and the views in your garden. You could try painting with watercolors, oil paint, or tempera paints; photography; pencil sketching; drawing with crayons or oil pastels; using only black and white; using only shades of green; drawing one part of a plant in a very close-up view; or drawing a landscape of your whole garden.

CHALKBOARD OBSERVATION STATION

CHALK IS A FAVORITE MATERIAL to use in the garden, throughout math, literacy, art, and play activities. Here's a way to include science, investigation, and writing with a chalkboard observation station.

MATERIALS

- Large chalkboard
- Chalk

You'll need a large chalkboard to create your observation station. You might use an actual board of wood painted with chalkboard paint or bring out a chalkboard from your indoor classroom. You can also use chalkboard paint to cover a surface in your garden, instantly giving you a place to write and draw—perhaps painting a garden door, the wall of your shed, or a section of your boundary fencing.

Wherever you choose to locate your chalkboard observation station, be sure to leave plenty of chalk alongside so the children have a way to record their findings. A plastic pot with a lid is a perfect place to store the chalks outdoors, whatever the weather.

The chalkboard then becomes a hub for gathering information about all the things going on in your garden. Write some headings or questions on your board as prompts for the children to write about their findings:

- Today the weather is...
- Today the season is...
- Today we saw...
- Today we smelled...
- Today we harvested...
- An unusual thing we saw today was...
- Creatures we spotted today include...

You might like to use paint or special markers to create permanent headings on your board or write them each time you use it. You can invite all the children to use the board whenever they see something they'd like to note down, or you could pick a different child each day to be the record keeper.

SENSORY-WORD HUNTING

THIS SENSORY-WORD ACTIVITY combines vocabulary building, reading, and writing with teamwork, sensory exploration, and some active running around.

MATERIALS

- Pieces of card stock
- Pens or pencils

In our sensory-word hunt we're going to think about all the words we can come up with to describe the sights, touch sensations, and smells in the garden.

Start by dividing the children into pairs or small groups and giving everyone some pieces of card stock and pens or pencils. Challenge them to think of sensory words to describe the things they can see, hear, feel, or taste in the garden. I find it helps to work with others when we're trying to think up suggestions for words, as it generates lots of ideas and avoids leaving anyone struggling alone to think of something. Write one of their words on each of their cards. Tell them the words will be part of a challenge for the other children, so to think up some great ones. Soft, spiky, rough, smooth, zingy, gentle, bumpy ... how does the garden classroom feel to them?

Then have each group gather its words together and swap them with another group. Each team now has a new set of words to look at. Can they read each of the words?

Next it's time for some active fun. Send each group off around your outside space looking for something that matches their words. Can they find something in the garden that is soft? If they can, they place the word card by the object or plant. The challenge is to find something to match each word. If they can't, the team that originally thought up the word must find something to match their word.

To finish off this activity, gather all the children together and go on a sensory walk around your garden. Walk from label to label and touch, listen to, smell, and perhaps taste each thing to see how it matches up with its sensory word.

As an extension activity, you might like to gather up your word labels and use them as a springboard to create a collaborative artwork, making a collage picture of your garden, including a variety of materials to reflect as many of the different sensory experiences as you can.

NATURE
—— TREASURE BAG ——

A NATURE TREASURE BAG combines art, literacy, and nature in a treasure-hunting adventure.

MATERIALS

- Painters' tape
- 2 pieces of paper or card stock
- Paint
- Paintbrush
- Stickers and colored pencils
- Laminating machine or contact paper
- Hole punch
- Ribbon or string

To make the treasure bag, first mark each child's initial with tape in the center of one of his or her pieces of card stock. Paint a design over this initial, so the tape is covered by the paint. You may also like to paint a design on one side of the other piece of card stock, so both sides of the finished bag are decorated. When the paint is dry, peel off the tape to reveal the artist's initial.

You can add some language learning by talking about all the things you might find on your nature walk. Include ideas for colors and textures you might discover. Write or draw your answers on some stickers and add them to one piece of card stock.

Laminate both pieces of card stock or cover them in contact paper to protect them. Put the two pieces together, design sides out, and use a hole punch to make holes around the two sides and the bottom edge of the sheets. More holes, close together, will mean none of the treasures will fall out of the bag.

Using ribbon or string, weave it through the holes, lacing the two pieces of card together, leaving some extra ribbon at the top to make a handle. Tie the loose ends with a knot, and your bag is ready to go.

Set off on a nature walk to see how many things you can find to match the words on your treasure bag. You might like to use the treasures you find to make a sticky picture (see page 171) or a leaf collage (see page 160).

JACK AND
—THE BEANSTALK—

JACK AND THE BEANSTALK is a great story to accompany some creative play in your garden. It offers the perfect, fun combination of adventure and triumph over adversity, with a good dash of horticulture thrown into the mix. A real beanstalk is easy to grow and a good plant to choose when gardening with children. The bean seeds are large, making them easy to handle, and they're reliable, so success is pretty much guaranteed. Plus, they grow very fast and tall; they're a delight to watch as they develop almost right before your eyes—just like Jack's beanstalk in the story. Bringing stories to life in this way helps to make reading so much more fun for children. We're enriching their experience by moving the tale from the pages of a book into a creative, developing, real-world experience full of sensory elements and play.

MATERIALS

- Pens and pencils
- Card stock
- Scissors
- Wooden sticks or skewers
- Clear tape
- Beanstalk, grown up a beanpole
- Clothespins
- Camera (optional)
- Garden journal (optional)

Start by making some puppets of the characters for your story. Use the pens and pencils to draw out Jack, his mother, and the giant on card stock. Add the cow and the golden goose and any other props you like. Cut them out and attach a wooden skewer to the back of each puppet with tape.

Then grow your beanstalk. French or runner beans are good choices when you're gardening with children, as the seeds are large and easy to handle. The likelihood of germination and successful growth is good, and as they grow quickly, they keep children interested, as they can see daily progress. They can also produce lots of beans to harvest, and the more you pick, the better chance there is that they will continue to grow.

Following the Planting Seeds guide on page 23 plant your bean seeds in a pot with some compost or plant them directly in the garden. Depending on the variety you've chosen, they're likely to start growing within a week or so, and you can support them with a beanpole as they get taller. Keep watering and watch your beanstalk grow and grow.

At each stage of the beanstalk's growth, you can use your puppets to act out the story. Have your Jack puppet help you plant the seeds. You can fix your puppets to the beanpole with clothespins. You can attach your giant puppet to the pole at the top of the beanstalk and position Jack up, up, up the beanstalk as he climbs. Just take a little care to pin the puppets only to the pole, not to the actual stalk of your beans, so you don't damage your plant.

As the children act out the story with their puppets, you can take photographs of each scene. Print out the photographs and include them in your garden journal, adding captions to each image to retell the story.

— STORY STONES —

STORY STONES PROVIDE another way to include creative play and storytelling in your garden space.

MATERIALS

- Paint, permanent markers, colored pencils, or crayons
- Selection of small stones and pebbles
- Clear varnish (optional)

To make a set of story stones to use to tell tales in the garden, you'll need to paint or draw some characters on your pebbles. Think about all the characters you might encounter in your garden storytelling. You might like to make a set of story stones to retell a fairy tale: a gingerbread man, an old man and lady, a cow, a horse, and a wily fox. You may want to draw figures that fit with a natural setting: a ladybug, a bee, a butterfly, and a caterpillar.

You also might like to include creatures from farther afield or from your imagination: a lion, a tiger, an elephant, and a dragon. It's useful to make some pebbles into props that can help to push your story along: a magic carpet, a tree, a map, a key, or a bottle of magic potion, perhaps.

Using acrylic paint will give you strong, clear images, but permanent markers, tempera paints, and crayons are perhaps less messy options. A layer of clear varnish over the surface of each pebble will help preserve your pictures, especially as the stones will be used outside and exposed to the elements.

As an alternative to permanent story stones, you could paint all of your pebbles with chalkboard paint and set them out in the garden with a pot of chalks. That way the children can draw whichever characters they would like to use in their story on a particular day and then rub off the chalk when they've finished playing, leaving the set of chalkboard stones blank and ready to use on another occasion.

When you've created your story stones, you can set them outside in a basket, ready to be included in play. Your children might enjoy using them as they play in the sandbox or water tub, and they can also play with them in the grass and flower beds. The character stones are good additions to a fairy garden, miniature garden, and dinosaur world too.

You can also use them in a more structured activity, bringing everyone together for a group story time. Gather everyone in the shade of a tree, in a tent filled with comfortable cushions, or around a fire pit or campfire and use the story stones as prompts to weave a tale. The simplest way to play, especially if you are with one or two children, is to pick a few of the stones and have them start a conversation among themselves, with you and your child providing the words. If you have a larger group, the children could each pick a stone and you could work your way around the gathering, with each person adding a sentence or two, bringing his or her stone character into the action. Or invite the children to pair up, pick a handful of stones, and prepare a story together to share with the group.

FAIRY OR
—GNOME MAILBOX—

A RATHER MAGICAL WAY to include some creative writing in your garden classroom is to set up a fairy or gnome mailbox. An activity such as this can encourage even reluctant writers to have a try: Who wouldn't like to receive a real magical letter? Checking the mailbox can become a regular part of your gardening routine, and letters and notes can be passed back and forth all year-round. The correspondence shows children that writing has a practical purpose, and a dash of magic and whimsy only makes it more fun.

MATERIALS

- Miniature mailbox, bought or homemade
- Selection of paper, envelopes, and postcards
- Pens and pencils
- Stickers
- Glitter

Find a spot in your garden to set up a miniature mailbox, perhaps under a bush or in the shade of a tree. You can use a bought mailbox or make your own from a plastic container. You can use this mailbox to send and receive letters to and from the fairies and gnomes who might live in your garden.

Set up a letter-writing station, either indoors or outside, and stock it with little sheets of writing paper, envelopes, and postcards. Add some fancy pens and pencils, with stickers to use as postage stamps. Invite your children to write some letters to the fairies and gnomes. They might like to tell them something about themselves or ask the fairies and gnomes questions about how they live in the garden. Where do they live? What do they eat? Are they friends with the butterflies? Fold up your letters and post them in the mailbox. Will you receive a reply? How wonderful it would be if the fairies and gnomes, or their adult assistants, wrote back and set up a garden pen pal scheme to last all year-round. Little gifts such as berries or useful twigs might be exchanged. And you might just see some traces of fairy-dust glitter too.

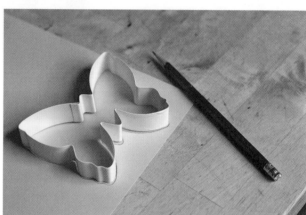

SCIENCE &
MATH

A GARDEN CLASSROOM CAN BRING a breath of fresh air to your science and math curriculum. Children who like these subjects will enjoy them anywhere, but going outdoors to the garden offers so much opportunity to make the learning more practical and more profound. And children who aren't engaged by math and science taught in a traditional classroom-based way may find that the change of scene to the outdoors transforms textbook lessons into meaningful, fun lessons that they can see the benefit of and enjoy. Have you heard the phrase "hands-on, brains on"? It emphasizes the idea that children learn best when they are taking part in active learning: when they are doing things, creating, using real materials, trying out activities for themselves, rather than only reading about something in a book or on a work sheet. A garden project abounds with opportunities for learning in a hands-on way.

We have already seen in the "Let's Grow! Garden Basics" chapter how gardening has inherent math and science as we count seeds, watch germination take place, and observe plants grow and produce flowers and fruit. In this chapter we will look more specifically at what we can do to focus on these subjects, both by using the intrinsic opportunities of the natural world and by introducing new materials and activities to boost learning. We will look at some key articles that we can provide for children to help them get the most learning from the environment, and we'll look at things we can make together, such as a bug hotel and a tree-trunk geoboard. We'll think about how we can take growing plants and use them as a springboard into conducting experiments that let us compare plants, test theories, and learn more about botany. I'll show you how you can equip an investigation table to promote child-directed inquiry and learning, and we'll also have some fun with ideas like a plant Olympics and minibeast bingo. Let's begin by thinking of ways we can equip our garden classroom to make it a place for natural scientific exploration.

SCIENCE IN THE GARDEN

Growing a garden with your children gives you a real, live science lab right outside your back door. Garden science is readily accessible, hands-on learning, with Mother Nature providing an ever-changing set of resources for you to explore, test, observe, and learn from. There's no need for any expensive equipment or a huge space to introduce some science lessons into your garden classroom: if you have a few seeds, some plant pots, and some soil, you're good to go. Here are a few other modest tools that can go a long way toward enriching your science study.

A SOIL-TESTING KIT

A soil-testing kit allows you to test how acid or alkaline your soil is, opening up opportunities to talk about soil structure and properties and different environments around the world.

A COMPOST BIN

As well as being a great way to recycle plant prunings and kitchen waste to make a compost that will really help your plants grow, a compost bin allows us to think about chemical and biological agents at work changing structures through decay, and how an ecosystem works.

A MAGNIFYING GLASS OR MICROSCOPE

A magnifying glass or a microscope will let you get up close to plants and bugs, helping you see their colors, texture, shape, and structure in much more detail.

GARDEN REFERENCE BOOKS

Having a selection of nature books available will allow your children to dip in and research and answer questions as they arise. Guides to your native insects and wildlife, a bird-watching book, and a plant encyclopedia are all useful.

A VARIETY OF PLANTS

Growing a selection of plants gives you a rich variety of types to study, compare, and contrast. Having some flowers, some fruit, and some vegetables opens up your science study to consider what similarities and differences each has, allowing children to deepen the knowledge they already have about gardens and also enriching their learning by introducing new aspects. The "five favorites" that I shared at the beginning of this book—potatoes, sunflowers, nasturtiums, lettuce, and tomatoes—offer a good range of learning possibilities. You'll also find that growing a variety of plants

will encourage many more types of insects and other wild animals into your garden classroom, bringing with them the chance to study them too.

We'll see later in this chapter how we can use plants to carry out experiments that explore growing conditions and plant development, but while we are thinking about stocking our garden classroom, let's also see how we can set it up to be a place for math learning as well.

MATH IN THE GARDEN

Simply starting and tending a garden with your children brings you everyday opportunities to work on math concepts: We learn about time as we follow the seasonal cycle of the planting year. We count the days between sowing seeds and germination, between planting and harvesting our first fruits. We work with area, geometry, and fractions as we plan which plants to grow in which section of our plot. We might decide to build a raised bed, measuring out a rectangle, checking that corners are true right angles, sectioning off a third for peas, a third for potatoes, and a third for lettuce. We meet multiplication as we plant seeds in pots. As we pop a couple of seeds into each section of a seed tray, we build a two, four, six, eight pattern as we sow. Every time we head out with a basket to collect that day's crop of peas or beans or tomatoes, we can count and add our produce totals. We practice division as we share fairly the harvest of strawberries among all the persons helping in the garden. We use volume as we fill watering cans, give half a can to each plant pot, or measure out the right amount of fertilizer to add to each watering. We work with three dimensions, shapes, and elevations as we build plant frames and tepees or build forts under trees.

All of this happens as we garden, whether we have a specific math curriculum in mind or not. Add some additional games and activities, and the garden classroom lets you teach a whole math syllabus outdoors. Let's look at some ideas we can use to supplement the math happening in the garden.

NATURAL MATH MANIPULATIVES

We know that especially with younger children in the early stages of learning math concepts, using hands-on manipulatives helps them understand the real significance of numbers and mathematical processes. In an indoor classroom we might use blocks, plastic beads, or bottle tops to count, make ten, and add amounts together. In our garden classroom we have a rich supply of natural materials to use as our hands-on resources. Items we might use in our garden classroom include leaves, twigs, pebbles, pinecones, pea pods, tomatoes, potatoes, petals, and flower heads.

MATH PEBBLES

You can also create a set of math pebbles for your games. Use permanent markers or paint to write on a series of pebbles. Write numbers on some and plus, minus, and equals signs on others. You can cover your pebbles with a layer of varnish to help protect them, particularly if you are going to leave them outdoors.

MATH GAMES FOR THE GARDEN

Any math concept you would be teaching indoors can work just as well outdoors—perhaps better, as playing with pea pods and flower petals feels, in both a sensory way and an emotional way, so very different from sitting at a desk with a work sheet.

- We can use chalk to write math puzzles on the school yard or driveway and use our pea pods to count out the answer. How many pea pods do we have together if you pick three and I pick four?
- We can call out number questions and have the children work out the solution with acorns. If a squirrel found two acorns yesterday and finds seven more today, how many does the squirrel have to add to its winter store?
- We can use leaves and twigs to work on concepts of units, tens, and hundreds. We can collect one hundred leaves from under the trees, then use a counting stick and thread ten leaves on the stick. How many more sticks do we need to make sets of ten to use up all one hundred leaves? Once you've made a set, you can practice skip counting in tens among your counting sticks.
- We can collect a variety of leaves in different colors and use them to explore patterns and number sequences. Let's begin a repeating pattern of two green leaves, two brown leaves, two green leaves, and two brown leaves and see how long a pattern we can make. Then let's see if we can skip count two, four, six, eight . . . all the way along the line.
- We can explore area by finding out how many pinecones we need to fill a space. We might draw a series of circles on the school yard or driveway with chalk—one big, one very large, and one in between. Can we guess how many pinecones we'd need to collect to fill each area? Then we can run around to collect enough to fill each space and count them to find the answer.

COUNTING TREASURE HUNT

For very young children, you can use the garden as a math treasure hunt. See if you can find one green leaf, two twigs, three yellow flowers, four pebbles, five pinecones, six pea pods. . . . Let the children enjoy running around the garden to find the treasures and

then bring them back to lay out in lines on the ground and count them. You can use your number pebbles to match with the corresponding lines.

ADDITION AND SUBTRACTION

Use your math pebbles to ask a series of math questions. Set out a number one pebble, a plus pebble, a three pebble, and an equals pebble and have the children add the correct four pebble at the end to complete your math sentence. Have a basket of sticks, pebbles, or pinecones available for the children to use to work out the answers if they need to. You can work in pairs to begin and complete math sentences together.

GRAPHING

Give the children two minutes to collect leaves from the ground and time them with a stopwatch. Bring back all the leaves you have gathered and use them to create a graph. Adapt your graph to suit the vegetation available in your plot, a park, or your garden. Do the children think there will be more green leaves or more yellow leaves? More oak leaves or more beech leaves? More narrow leaves or more broad leaves?

Lay the leaves out on the ground to create a bar chart: make a tall line of green leaves, then next to this a tall line of yellow leaves, then next to this a tall line of brown leaves, for example. This gives you a clear set of bars on your graph so you can count the number of leaves on each bar and compare your results.

SUNFLOWERS:
—— A COMPLETE SCIENCE STUDY ——

Simply growing a sunflower with your child gives you a whole year of science study.

In spring we get to learn about seeds and germination and find out what things seeds need to grow well. We can study the parts of a plant as they emerge, observing their progress, sketching them, researching their correct names, and learning a new vocabulary.

In summer we can measure how tall the stems grow, tracking progress weekly and graphing our results. We can note how the flower heads begin to appear, how each one peels open to reveal the complex interior. We can draw, photograph, and paint our own pictures of the glorious flowers and compare and contrast them with other plants around the garden. We can study the bees and butterflies that visit the sunflowers and learn about pollen and nectar and pollination. We can wonder why sunflowers turn their faces during the course of the day and research the movement of the earth and the sun.

In autumn we can observe how the flower heads change and use a magnifying glass to see close up the seeds inside. We might see the plants droop their heads toward the soil, ready to drop seeds, and we can hypothesize about how different plants have adapted to make the dispersal of their seeds more successful.

In winter we can complete our study of the sunflower cycle and learn that some plants are annuals, some biennials, and some perennials. We can survey which birds visit our garden to feed on the nutritious seeds within the sunflower heads, and we can research how other animals find food sources over the winter months. We can harvest some of the seeds ourselves to plant next year and begin the annual cycle again, and we can discuss ideas of sustainability and self-sufficiency.

All of this science study from just a few seeds and one type of plant. Think of the possibilities that abound as you develop your garden classroom over time.

INVESTIGATION TABLE

EVERY GARDEN CLASSROOM should have an investigation table. It's a place to gather together some of the interesting finds from around your outdoor space for closer study and exploration.

Give some thought to the location of your nature table. You'll want it to be somewhere that is readily available to the children so they notice it and use it often—rather than tucking it away in a forgotten corner. You might like to have your table indoors so you can bring items in from your outdoor classroom to look at alongside books and other resources. If you have a covered area in your garden—under a shelter, in a shed, or within a tent or fort—an outdoor investigation table allows the children to discover more about the plants and creatures they come across as soon as they find them. And if you are able to have a table indoors and out, even better. A great investigation table might include an array of tools:

> Items collected from your garden classroom: fruit, vegetables, plants, flowers, insects and other creatures, and other found natural materials such as twigs, leaves, pebbles, and feathers

> Books for research and inspiration: information books on local plants and animals; books about contrasting natural environments around the world; story- and poetry books featuring garden settings, plants, and animal characters

> Writing materials: garden journals, clipboards, paper and card stock, pens, and pencils. These materials will encourage children to write, draw, and record their findings

> A camera: children can photograph their discoveries, and the photos they take can be displayed on their investigation table, included in their garden journals, and used to make photo diaries

> A microscope or magnifying glass: these tools help children look at plants and animals up close

> Discovery boxes: boxes containing a contrasting variety of natural materials, to compare and contrast

Transparent plastic boxes with lids: plastic boxes can be used as specimen cases that hold insects and other creatures for a short period of time for closer study.

Art materials: paper, canvases, an easel, paints (tempera, oil, and watercolors), pencils, crayons, and oil pastels. These tools enable children to capture the beauty of the garden through their own art. Also, set up a bulletin board or string up a clothesline so the children can display their art around the investigation table.

Once your investigation table is set up, it can be a place to explore the treasures from the garden in much more detail. Here are a few examples:

- Take time to observe things, noticing how they grow, change, and develop.
- Compare items, noting differences in color, texture, and size.
- Research information about the items you collected.
- Photograph, sketch, and paint things you've found.
- Make notes in your garden journals.
- Celebrate the produce and beauty of your garden classroom.

GROWING SEEDS EXPERIMENT: PART ONE

GROWING PLANTS FROM SEED is a perfect way for children to see science in action and to conduct hands-on experiments. Pick a reliable seed that will germinate quite quickly, such as beans or sunflowers, and follow these ideas as you plant to discover what a seed really needs in order to grow.

MATERIALS

- Seeds
- Compost
- Seed trays or small plant pots

Start by taking a good look at the seeds and taking a photograph or drawing them to add to your garden journal. How big are they? What color? Take a look at the compost or soil, too, and talk about how it feels in your hand. Note the words the children think of to describe the soil: Is it warm, heavy, crumbly, thick?

Use a seed tray or several small plant pots to plant your seeds. Follow the planting guide in the Planting Seeds section on page 23 and count your seeds as you plant. Add some writing practice by making plant labels. It's good for young children to understand that writing has a very practical purpose—and making sure you remember what you've planted where is very important. However young the child is, let her or him make an attempt at writing the plant's name on the label. With older children you might like to talk about how the plant gets its scientific name.

Now for some experimenting. Ask the children what they think a seed needs to grow—and test their ideas. Try growing some seeds in the dark. Try growing some without any water. Will they grow in the freezer? Or in a warm spot? See if a few seeds will grow just in a pot of water, without any compost. Use your garden journal to record your results and see if you can discover the very best place to grow a seed.

GROWING SEEDS EXPERIMENT: PART TWO

IT'S INTERESTING FOR CHILDREN to understand that not all plants grow in the same way. This experiment takes a closer look at germination and compares two different types of seed, measuring and charting their growing progress. It puts the children in charge of designing the experiment and includes lots of opportunity for math and literacy work.

Bean and pea seeds work well for this experiment. They're large, which makes them easy to handle, and the different shapes make them an interesting contrast. They germinate quickly, too, giving the children something to see without having to wait too long. To enhance the experiment, you can also watch plant cuttings and potatoes growing, comparing their development with what you are observing in your seed-growing exercise.

MATERIALS

- Clear glass cup or plastic container
- Cotton balls
- Bean and pea seeds
- Plant cuttings (optional)
- Potatoes (optional)

Fill two glasses with cotton balls to act as the soil and dampen the cotton balls with water. Pop a pea seed in one glass, and a bean seed in the other, placing them at the edge of the glass to get a good view of them as they begin to grow. Check your seeds each day to see their progress. Keep the pot moist but not too soggy, and watch as the roots begin to grow. How do they know to grow downward? What happens to the roots if you turn your seeds upside down?

Next come the first leaves, not actually true leaves but cotyledons, which will wither and die as the real leaves appear. Turn your observatory away from the sunlight and see what happens to the stem of your plant.

Ask the children to decide what they would like to measure. You might choose to chart any of the following:

- How long it takes for the seeds to begin to grow
- How long before there is a leaf
- How long before there is a flower

- Which seed variety grows to four inches first
- How long it takes until you have something you can eat

Ask the children to predict the answers to their questions. Then decide how to record your results. You might like to use your garden journal to keep photographs or draw the changes each day. You might like to record the days in a tally or a bar chart. Having two different types of seeds in the experiment lets you compare results.

COMPARING YOUR SEEDLINGS WITH PLANT CUTTINGS AND POTATOES

To contrast what you have observed in the growth of your seeds, it is interesting to take a closer look at plant cuttings and potatoes.

Try taking some plant cuttings and growing them in your observatory to see how they root and become a whole new plant. Spider plants, *Chlorophytum comosum,* are great for this experiment, and you can start cuttings successfully in just a glass of water, which gives you the opportunity to see the roots clearly.

What about trying potatoes in an observatory? A tall, clear plastic bottle, such as a soda bottle, is a good shape and size for this. Place some compost at the bottom and set your seed potato on top, close to the edge of the bottle, so growth will be visible. Watch how the eyes begin to sprout and leaves appear. Keep watching, and roots will grow from the bottom of your potato. As the leaves grow up inside your observatory, keep filling it up with more compost, covering right over all the leaves until they've grown up to the very top of the bottle. Then watch, and you might spot brand-new potatoes appearing inside the bottle.

(*Note:* The potatoes used in this experiment are not suitable for eating, as they have been exposed to daylight and may develop green patches, making them harmful to eat. Plant another crop of potatoes outside in the soil and keep these observatory ones just for your experiment.)

— MINIBEAST BINGO —

GARDEN CREATURES ARE FASCINATING to young children, often stopping them in their tracks as they pause to peer at an ant trail or a spiderweb. This idea for minibeast bingo encourages children to observe carefully and chart all the different inhabitants of their garden.

MATERIALS

- Pens and pencils
- Animal reference book
- Scissors
- Glue
- Card stock and paper

Begin by talking about what animals you might expect to see in your habitat and then draw pictures of them. Everyone can join in on this, drawing from memory or imagination or copying from reference books.

Cut out and stick all of your animal and insect pictures on a big piece of card stock and write the creatures' names underneath each one. Every time you spot a new creature in the garden, you can tick it off your chart. You might like to go on a minibeast hunt or watch for them as you garden and play.

Take time to have a good look at each animal as you find it. Observe its shape, color, and patterns and count its legs. Talk about its role in the garden ecosystem and decide whether it is a goody or a baddy.

If you like a competition, you could make each child a slightly different bingo card to see who can spot all of the creatures first to get a full card. Or promote harmony in the garden with one big bingo card to complete together.

BIRD CAFÉ

ANOTHER ON-YOUR-DOORSTEP science project a garden classroom affords is the study of the birds that visit. You can focus on the species that are native to where you live, perhaps contrasting them with a study of birds from a different part of the world. You can also follow the cycle of the birds' year, watching for changes in their activity: when they are gathering twigs to make nests, when they begin collecting worms to feed their young, and when you spot them emerging with chicks that are beginning to fledge. If you put up birdhouses, you might be lucky enough to be blessed with birds nesting in your garden, but you can also encourage birds to visit with the following ideas for creating a bird café. Use the recipes to set up a feeding station, then sit and watch the birds come and eat. You could keep a record of which birds visit by taking photographs or drawing sketches to add to your garden journal, and use reference books to learn facts about each species.

POPCORN CHAINS

String some popcorn chains to wind around a tree and deck your garden with bird-friendly bunting. To make a chain, pop some corn kernels (with no added salt or sugar), then use a needle to string them on some thread. Wrap the chain around a tree or bush in your garden, tying down each end so your chain doesn't blow away. You can add raisins and dried cranberries to give the birds an extra treat.

MAKE A SEED CAFÉ

This seedcake recipe offers birds a rich and nutritious food mix that is especially beneficial to them in cold winter months and when they are preparing to lay eggs. Mix it up and offer it in a pot with built-in perches, creating a café for the birds in your garden.

Take a small plastic pot and use a craft knife to make a small hole in the bottom. Find two sticks to make perches—twigs, lollipop sticks, and kebab skewers all work well. Cross the two sticks to make an *X* and secure the intersection of the two sticks with a little transparent tape. Thread some string through the hole in the bottom of your pot, around the sticks at the top, and back through the hole in the bottom again. This holds the sticks in place, and the string ends can be tied together to form a loop for hanging the feeder from a tree branch.

Make your bird feed using the seedcake recipe on the next page. Pack the seed mix into your plastic pot and press it down well. Let it chill and harden in the fridge for an hour or so. Once hard, press the sides of the plastic pot to release the seed cake, and remove the plastic pot. Hang your seed café from the branch of a tree in your garden where you can see it clearly from where you play.

SEEDCAKE RECIPE

Mix one part lard with two parts birdseed. You can also add raisins, peanuts, dried cranberries, or grated cheese. You can use a spoon to mix it or squish it all together with your hands. Do not melt the lard (or it will run out through the hole in your plastic pot) but have it at room temperature so it's easy to combine with the seeds.

CREATURES CLOSE UP

YOUR GARDEN OFFERS children the chance to get up close to lots of wild animals: to study how they look and how they move, to find out where they live and what they eat, and to begin to understand how the garden is one whole community where your children and the tiniest ladybug both have a home and a purpose. Take advantage of your backyard zoo and go on a beast hunt to observe these creatures close-up.

SET A TRAP

Setting up a simple bug trap overnight lets you take a closer look at the creatures that come out after you've gone to sleep.

Use a small plastic container such as a yogurt pot and set it down in the soil so the rim is level with the top of your soil. Prop a cover over the top of the trap so animals can pass beneath it but your trap will not fill up with any rain. Add a few leaves or some grass clippings to the bottom of your trap, then leave it overnight.

In the morning you might find you have been rewarded by some visitors. Use a magnifying glass to take a close look and see if you can identify the creatures you have caught. Treat the animals very carefully, and be sure to release them back into the wild as soon as you have had a good look.

ZOOM IN

Use a magnifying glass to zoom right in and take an extraclose look at the creatures in your garden. Look under logs, turn over leaves, or best of all, see if you can find a bug crawling up a windowpane or inside a jam jar. What details of the animals can you see when you get really close?

If you have a camera with a macro setting, switch to that view—you'll get amazing results and help your children to learn about the animals in much more detail. See the mouth of a snail or the intricate details on the wings of a fly. You can also use your camera to document changes in your garden journal, recording how leaves unfurl or flower buds open. The picture here shows cabbage white butterfly eggs developing on the leaf of a nasturtium plant and gives the children a view that's hard to see with just the human eye.

CREATE A WILDLIFE HAVEN

There are simple steps you can take to make your garden a paradise for bugs and beasts:

- Grow a wide variety of plants to provide food all through the year.
- Include lots of nectar-rich flowers with large daisy-style blooms.
- Don't be too tidy—leave piles of leaves to provide homes and shelter.
- Include native plants and wildflowers in your planting scheme.
- Set up a bug hotel (see the next project) for overwintering animals.
- Create a bird café to provide an important extra source of food for birds.
- Set up a small woodpile to provide food and shelter.

BUG HOTEL

CREATE A COZY HABITAT for insects to shelter in during the winter by making a bug hotel.

MATERIALS

- Framework for your hotel: wood and bricks, pallets, crates, boxes
- Plastic mesh
- Selection of materials to fill the hotel (see suggestions below)
- Paper tubes and flowerpots

You can make a bug hotel for overwintering insects from planks of wood layered on bricks, pallets, or crates. A small shelving unit or a storage box tipped on its side with the bottom removed works well too. Stapling plastic mesh on the back will keep the materials from slipping out as the hotel is filled but will still allow the bugs access to their new home.

Once you've made your structure, you need to fill the hotel with insect-friendly material suitable for making nests and sheltering. Talk with your children about the kinds of creatures that are likely to be living in your garden and why they are important. Ask the children to imagine they are a bee or a beetle and think about what they'd use to make a cozy bedroom. Try to use natural materials or recycled ingredients for your bug hotel so it costs nothing to make and is ecofriendly. Items to include could be bamboo poles, moss, dry leaves, logs, pebbles, slates, twigs, feathers, pinecones, bark, grasses such as pampas, and shredded paper.

Using paper tubes and flowerpots to make small chambers means every child can make his or her own chamber and add it to the bug hotel. When the bug hotel is filled, place it outside in a sheltered spot, ready and waiting for its first guests to check in. You might notice some of the bamboo poles get sealed up with a leaf plug, as hibernating bees make a home inside and close the door behind themselves.

LADYBUG
NUMBER LINE

A SET OF COUNTING LADYBUGS makes a perfect number line for young children. Ladybugs with their spots lend themselves to counting games very well, and the addition of stickers makes math even more fun.

MATERIALS

- Scissors
- Card stock
- Markers
- Clothesline made from string and clothespins
- Dot stickers

To start your ladybug counting line, first make your ladybugs. Cut out some ladybug shapes from red card stock and color in black heads, but do not add spots at this stage. Write the numbers one through ten on them. Hang them up with clothespins on a clothesline and you're ready to count. You can hang your number line indoors or in the garden. Laminating the ladybugs will help protect them if they're going outside.

Let the children play with the ladybugs and use them for some counting games.

- Can you find the ladybug with a number one?
- Can you apply the right number of stickers to match the number?
- Which ladybug has the most stickers?
- Can you line up the ladybugs from one to ten or from ten to one?
- This ladybug has two spots—can you find a ladybug with one more spot?
- How old are you? Can you find a ladybug with the same number of spots?

ONE-YARD
LEAF RACE

TO INTRODUCE SOME MEASUREMENT into your garden learning, play the one-yard leaf race. This game combines fun gross-motor active play, as the children run around, with accurate measuring and plant identification and classification—all with a little competition challenge thrown in for fun.

MATERIALS

- Tape measures or yardsticks
- Leaves

This game works well all year-round but is perhaps at its most glorious in autumn, when you have a rich variety of leaf colors available. It's up to you whether you have a rule that only leaves that have already fallen to the ground can be collected or whether the children are allowed to pick leaves directly from the plants.

The aim of the game is to race to collect a set of leaves that measure a total of one yard when laid end to end. Divide the children into a number of teams. Allocate each team a particular type of leaf that they must collect. The easiest way to play the game is to differentiate by color, so one team collects green leaves, another collects brown, and so on, but as your young gardeners develop their plant knowledge, you might like to work with plant species and have one team collect oak leaves and another collect birch, for example.

Lay out the tape measures on the ground, with one available for each team, and have the children identify how long one yard is.

Then you're off, and each team has to race to collect enough leaves to lay them out in a line to reach their mark. You might like to work against a stopwatch or declare the first team to make a yard of leaves the winner.

HOST A PLANT OLYMPICS

TO BRING LOTS OF COUNTING, measuring, and weighing into your garden, you can host a fruit and vegetable Olympics to see who the champion growers of the year are. Hosting a plant Olympics is a fun way to include lots of math in your garden as you harvest the fruit and vegetables you have been growing.

MATERIALS

- Fruit and vegetables from the garden
- Tape measures or rulers
- Weighing scales
- Clipboards and paper or chalkboard
- Pens, pencils, or chalk
- Card stock

Help the children to organize a survey of your garden produce to measure and weigh the different fruits and vegetables. Discuss how you are going to measure each category and collate your results to find the winners. Use clipboards and paper and pencils or a chalkboard and chalk to note the results. You could show your findings in graphs, charts, or tables. Design some certificates and medals on card stock to award to the winners.

You might like to have the children compete to find the following produce:

- Tallest sunflower
- Sunflower head with the biggest diameter
- Heaviest squash
- Pumpkin with the biggest circumference
- Longest carrot
- Potato that covers the biggest area
- Pea pod that contains the most peas

SUNFLOWER HEIGHT CHART

SUNFLOWERS ARE A VERY SUITABLE plant for children to grow, as the seeds are reliable, the plants grow very quickly and can tower above children's heads, and the flower heads are so beautiful. Combining them with this height chart invites your children to observe a sunflower's growth carefully, measuring, counting, and comparing progress and then graphing the results.

MATERIALS

- Markers or pencils
- Green card stock
- Scissors
- Long roll of paper
- Tape
- Tape measure
- Sunflower seedling
- Handprint sunflower (see page 150; optional)

Start by having each child draw a leaf on green card stock, write her or his name on it, and cut it out.

Take a long roll of paper and tape it up on the wall, a door, or the side of the fridge. Draw a tall sunflower stalk up the roll of paper. Have each child stand against it and use the leaf with the child's name on it to mark how tall the child is. Talk about who is big, small, and medium and about how children and plants grow taller but adults do not.

Then it's the sunflower's turn. Measure a seedling with a tape measure to find out how tall it is. On the sunflower height chart measure out the height of the seedling and color in the stalk up to that level. You can add the date if you like.

Keep on measuring your sunflower as it grows and grows, charting its progress on your height chart. Will it grow bigger than the tallest person? At the end of the summer be sure to measure the children again, to see if they've grown over the months too.

The handprint sunflower art later in this book works well in combination with the height chart, giving you a grand finale to add to the top of your stalk.

SYMMETRY BUTTERFLIES

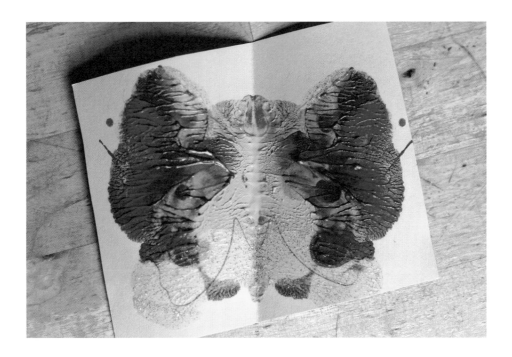

CREATING BUTTERFLY ART is a wonderful opportunity to explore symmetry with your children. Here's a classic children's craft idea to bring some magic to your painting.

MATERIALS

- Card stock
- Pen or pencil
- Paints
- Paintbrushes and sponges
- Glitter (optional)
- Scissors

Take a piece of card stock and draw the outline of a butterfly. You can make lots of butterflies in different shapes and sizes.

Fold the card in half, open it out, and then add some paint to just one butterfly half. This art is open to all children, even babies, as they can finger paint, smear color around, make handprints, or use brushes or sponges to apply the paint.

Now for the magic. Fold over your butterfly so the paint is on the inside of the card. Rub over the top of the card to squish and spread the paint around. Gently peel open the folded card to reveal the magic pattern across both the butterfly wings. You can add a shimmer of glitter while the paint is still wet.

Once the paint is dry, cut out your butterfly and use one of the following methods to finish it:

- Fix your butterfly to a greeting card.
- Add a paper clip on the back of your butterfly, using tape, to create a bookmark.
- Glue a miniclothespin to the back of the butterfly and pin it up.
- Add a pin to the butterfly to make a brooch.
- String up your butterflies to create a mobile in the house or across the branches of a tree.

TREE-TRUNK GEOBOARD

A GEOBOARD IS a learning tool that can be used with children of a wide variety of ages and stages to work on the areas of math that are suited to their individual progress. A geoboard made from a tree trunk is a great addition to your garden classroom, giving your children an interesting invitation to explore shape, geometry, and angles.

MATERIALS

- Section from a tree trunk
- Ruler and pencil
- Hammer and flat-head nails or pushpins
- Rubber bands of various colors

Make a square lattice of nails in your tree trunk: Use your ruler and pencil to mark the position for your nails to make a square lattice of nine, sixteen, or twenty-five (or more) nails. Then hammer in one nail or place a pushpin at each mark on your lattice ensuring each nail or pushpin remains sufficiently raised to allow you to put on the rubber bands. This gives you your geoboard grid.

Place the geoboard in a suitable location, perhaps on a table rather than on the floor, where children could fall on it. Provide a basket of rubber bands alongside the geoboard so the children can play and investigate the shapes they can make by wrapping the bands around the nails or pushpins on the board.

With any new learning equipment, it's good to allow the children simply to play with the materials first. This lets them explore the properties, ponder questions of their own, and make their own discoveries. When you are ready to explore the geoboard with some more-structured activities, there are many ways you can use it:

Making shapes: Can you use the rubber bands to make a square, a rectangle, a triangle … on the nails or pushpins?

Counting: How many different squares can you fit on the geoboard?

Repeating patterns: Can you use the different colors of your rubber bands to make repeating patterns across your geoboard?

Rotating shapes: Can you make a triangle in one section of the geoboard and then create another one in a different section, making the triangle exactly the same size but rotated 90 degrees?

Exploring symmetry: Make a design on one half of the geoboard and challenge your child to duplicate the design to make a symmetrical copy on the other half. In a class, you can pair up children and have them work together to make a symmetrical design.

Re-creating designs: Make a pattern on the geoboard and take a photograph of it. Print the image and use that picture as a challenge card. Can your child re-create the photographed design on the tree-trunk geoboard, copying the shapes, location, and colors of the rubber bands?

Exploring angles: Can you make a triangle with equal angles? Can you make a right-angled triangle? Can you make a triangle with an obtuse angle? And with an acute angle?

Exploring scale: Make a small square in one corner of the geoboard. Can you make another one on a bigger scale? Can you make one on an even bigger scale?

Measuring areas: Make a shape with rubber bands. Can you calculate the area of your shape, using a ruler to measure the lengths of the sides? Can you make a second shape that has the same area as your first design?

Measuring perimeter: Make another shape with the rubber bands. Can you measure the perimeter with a ruler? Can you make a different shape that has the same perimeter as the first?

ARTS & CRAFTS

YOU MAY NOT BE ABLE TO RIVAL nature's beauty, but you can take much inspiration from your garden to encourage your children to draw, paint, and craft. Finding opportunities for art in your classroom is just as important as including math, literacy, and science. Through painting, drawing, and creating, children are able to think creatively, try new things, and develop important skills. They work on fine-motor practice as they paint, draw, and finger knit. They discover the science of using different materials for different projects. They work with shapes, planes, and two and three dimensions. But in addition to these important skills, there is much more that arts and crafts offer them. They learn about themselves as they select colors and draw images that mean something special to them. They experiment, take risks, and dare to try new things. They meet the spirit, the holy, and the beauty of a garden and begin to translate that into thought, pictures, and forms. They find their voice, persevere, and innovate.

In this chapter you will find all sorts of art and craft projects you can try with children of all ages. You might like to invite them to flick through the images, to pick some ideas that they would like to explore for themselves. There are projects that take inspiration from the beauty in your garden and ones that make use of the real art materials your garden gives you. All of the activities can be done by children on their own, but many of them make wonderful collaborative projects, too, and can be a great way to come together and enjoy the community a garden co-op can offer.

Many of the projects also link well with the activities in the math, science, play, and literacy sections of this book, allowing you to weave the arts through your lessons and thus maximize the benefits of overlapping subjects and come to learning from many angles. If you have grown sunflowers as a hands-on gardening experience, studied their development in your science lesson, and written about them in your garden journals, now you will find here ideas to explore the natural beauty of them too. Using the hand-print sunflower idea to top your plant-growth chart is a wonderful project that combines math, science, art, sensory play, and collaborative teamwork. The caterpillar and butterfly ideas link well to the small-world play activities and scientific study of bugs and beasts. You will also find projects that introduce new materials and skills to your children. There are ideas for painting, printing, paper crafting, using cement, sewing, finger knitting, land art, and cooking. I include a fun twist on a traditional scarecrow and art projects that celebrate the beauty of your garden.

ART IN THE GARDEN

Your garden itself offers an interesting variety of art materials, including things to use as paintbrushes and ingredients to make DIY paint. The earliest known forms of human art were made using natural materials found in the immediate environment. From engraved sticks in Blombos Cave, South Africa, through cave paintings in Ubirr, Australia, and Chauvet Cave in Ardèche, France, to the land art in Nazca, Peru, there is a rich and interesting history of natural and land art you can study with your children. Then combine this inspiration with the ideas in this chapter and have a try at creating your own organic masterpieces.

CHALK IN THE GARDEN

One of the simplest ways to make art instantly available in the garden is to provide chalk for your children. Chalk in the garden is the ideal writing and drawing material. It can be used on walls, doors, patios, driveways, and even tree trunks—and it will all be washed away by rain or a watering can when you're finished. Keep a covered pot of chalk by the back door or hung from the handle of the shed, and your children can grab it any time they choose.

Here are some ideas for using chalk in the garden:

- Copy the shapes of creatures you discover.
- Write out messages for others to read.

- Lie down and draw around yourself.
- Mark out a street map and create a town in your garden.
- Draw large shapes and put numbers or sight words within them and toss a beanbag to see if you can hit a target number or word.
- Use free-style patchworks, swirls, and patterns to create some pavement art.
- Draw a grid and play hopscotch.

MAKE A SET OF GARDEN PAINTBRUSHES

To make a set of nature brushes, gather some materials from around the garden that you could paint with—some leaves, flowers, or seed heads. Take a stick to be your paintbrush and use some string to fasten your natural materials to the end as the tip of your brush. Use a variety of materials to create a set of brushes with different textures and tips.

Flowers on long stems can be used as paintbrushes just as they are. You can also dip the flower heads into paint and use them to make prints.

PAINT FROM YOUR GARDEN

Mud makes excellent paint, especially if you have a selection of different soil types that can give you different shades. You can also crush berries to make paint: try blackberries, strawberries, and raspberries. Or use some of your homegrown herbs to bring an additional sensory element to your art: chop up fresh herbs and add them to paint to add scent to your art. Let your green paint smell like mint and your purple smell like lavender.

Arts and crafts inspired by your garden classroom are a wonderful way to bring the outdoors in and create a connection between the different play and learning spaces in your home or school. Let's look at some projects you can try throughout the year, incorporating new materials and different techniques but all inspired by your garden space.

MAKING NATURAL PLANT DYES

Try using some of the plants in your garden to make natural dyes for art and craft projects. The colors will vary in strength and hue, depending on the plants themselves, so experiment and see what shades you can create.

PLANTS TO TRY

Yellow, brown, or red onion skins

Beet

Red cabbage

Strawberries

Rose petals

Celery leaves

Blueberries

Marigolds

Carrots

Blackberries

Lavender

TO MAKE YOUR PLANT DYE

Chop or shred your plant material. Place it in a saucepan with twice as much water as plant material (so, two cups of water for every one cup of plant material, for example). Simmer on a low heat for thirty minutes to an hour, until the water takes on the color from the plant. Allow the water to cool, leaving it overnight if you would like to develop a stronger color. Then strain the dye into a bowl.

USING YOUR DYE

You can use your natural dye for painting, or try coloring some eggs. Place a hard-boiled egg or a blown eggshell in the dye, using enough dye to cover the egg. Add one tablespoon of vinegar for every cup of dye you are using, as a fixative. Leave the egg in the dye for several hours, or overnight, for the color to develop on the egg. As a variation, you can wrap rubber bands around the eggs before placing them in the dye, to see what patterns you can create.

HANDPRINT
SUNFLOWER

MAKING A HANDPRINT sunflower is a wonderful collaborative project, as you can use the handprints of a whole class or family to make the petals.

MATERIALS

- Paper
- Yellow paint
- Scissors
- Stapler and glue
- Paper plate
- Black tissue paper or sunflower seeds

To make your sunflower, dip your hands in yellow paint and make lots of hand-prints on paper. Cut them out and then staple them around the edges of a paper plate. Scrunch up some black tissue paper, or use some real sunflower seeds, and glue the tissue paper or seeds to the center of your handprint flower.

The finished sunflower looks beautiful as a work of art and also makes a great topper for the sunflower height chart.

— CEMENT-TILE ART —

CEMENT TILES CREATE a beautiful, long-lasting art display in the garden. You can combine them with a variety of materials to make unique designs. The one in this photograph was made by the members of a school gardening club and uses a collection of recycled materials. You could also gather souvenirs from a woodland walk or a trip to the beach and use them to make a keepsake work of art to remember your visit.

MATERIALS

- Shoe-box lid
- Plastic bag
- Cement mix and water
- Tubular pasta
- Embellishments such as found, natural, and recycled items (see suggestions below)

Use an old shoe-box lid as a mold, lining it with a plastic bag. Mix up the cement according to its instructions, to a fairly thick consistency, then fill the shoe-box lid and smooth down the surface.

Insert pasta tubes in the wet cement to create holes to hang the tile in a gallery when you're finished. Leave the pasta in place for about two hours and then gently pull the tubes out to create the hanging holes.

At the same time as you insert the pasta tubes, and while the cement is still damp, embellish your tile with found items, natural materials, and recycled items. Push them gently into the wet cement, and they will fix in place. Try driftwood, twigs, shells, slate, beads from broken necklaces, buttons, bottle tops, pen lids, smooth glass, and feathers. Leave your tile exactly where it is for a few days to dry out and set hard. Then use garden twine or ribbon to hang your art in an outside gallery.

GARDEN BUNTING

BUNTING IS A BEAUTIFUL addition to a garden, bringing a party atmosphere and adding color all year-round, even when there are few plants growing. You can make your bunting in different ways, depending on whether it will be under cover or out in the elements. It's great as a group project for a family or a class, as everyone can contribute a panel to add to the chain of flags.

MATERIALS

- Card stock or fabric
- Scissors
- String or ribbon
- Stapler
- Sewing thread and needle
- Embellishments: fabric paint, other paints, scraps of fabric, buttons, sequins, leaves for printing
- Paintbrushes and/or sponges
- Fabric glue

If your bunting is going to be under cover or you're just decking out the garden for a party or special occasion, you can make it from card stock. Simply cut out triangles or rectangles, decorate them, and fasten them to lengths of string or ribbon using staples, for instant garden style.

To make bunting that can be out in the garden whatever the weather, use fabric. A thick calico will give you robust flags, whereas a thinner cotton will give more movement in the breeze, so pick your fabric to suit your needs. You might like to use fabric all in one color to unify your design or mix and match colors and patterns along your chain. Using your children's old clothes results in a beautiful keepsake set of bunting.

To make each flag, cut out a triangle or rectangle of fabric, then fold over a seam at the top and sew it in place with a simple running stitch. This gives you a tube at the top through which you can thread the string or ribbon for attaching your flags to the bunting.

Then decide on your style and decorate your flags. You might like to paint with handprints, paintbrushes, or sponges. Use fabric paint if you're making bunting on cloth. You could also cut the flags from art your children have already made.

Or take inspiration from the garden itself and make leaf prints along your bunting. Choose leaves of different shapes and sizes and paint a layer of paint on one side. Carefully press the leaf, paint side down, on your bunting, then peel off the leaf to reveal your prints.

You could create a letter on each flag to spell out a welcome or other message. Or use fabric scraps to make collages, adding buttons and sequins for extra embellishments. You can stitch the fabric in place or use fabric glue for a quicker option.

Once all paint and glue is dry, deck your garden with your bunting, hanging it across walls, gates, or tepees or from trees and umbrellas.

FINGER KNIT
A FLOWER

HAVE YOU EVER TRIED finger knitting? It's a simple technique and a suitable introduction to knitting for young children who find needles a little difficult to handle. It's very good fine-motor practice for nimble fingers and produces a satisfyingly quick chain of stitches. Follow these simple steps and you can make a pretty flower brooch so you can carry a memento of your garden with you wherever you go. The thickness of your yarn and the length of your chain will determine how big your brooch will be. This nine-inch-long chain turned into a brooch that is two inches in diameter.

MATERIALS

- Yarn
- Needle and thread
- Beads (optional)
- Brooch pin

To finger knit, you'll use the index finger of one hand as the needle. Your other hand (whichever one you'd use to write with) will wrap the yarn around and make the stitches.

Start by making a looped knot in the yarn and then place this first loop over your index finger. Use your other hand to wrap the yarn around your finger to make a second loop in front of the first. Pull the first loop over the second loop to slip it off and you've created your first stitch.

Make another loop around your finger. Pull the first loop over the second and you've made your next stitch. Keep looping and slipping off stitches and watch your chain grow. You might like to wrap the yarn twice around your finger for each stitch to produce a thicker chain and a chunkier brooch.

When you have finger knitted your chain, roll it up in a spiral like a snail shell to make your brooch. Then use a needle and thread (in a color that matches your yarn) to sew a few stitches through the brooch to hold it all together. You can sew so that all the stitches are on the back of the brooch, or you can sew them on the front and thread on a tiny bead every so often to give your brooch some extra sparkle.

Finally, on the reverse side, stitch on a brooch pin and you're done. The brooch looks good fastened to a piece of card or placed in a gift box if you're giving it as a gift and is great for brightening up coats, hats, scarves, and bags.

LEAF COLLAGE

CREATING LEAF COLLAGES lets children explore the shapes, textures, and colors of natural materials and use them in imaginative ways. Go for a walk around the garden, collect some natural art materials, and see what pictures you can create with them.

MATERIALS

- Contact paper
- Leaves and twigs
- Colored card stock (optional)
- Glue or transparent tape (optional)

Spread out a sheet of transparent contact paper and use the sticky side as the canvas to place your leaves on and create your art. You could make animals, garden pictures, or layered patterns. Using contact paper lets the children place and change the materials. You could tape a large sheet of contact paper to the outside of a windowpane so the children can add to the picture over time as they find more materials in the garden.

Alternatively, use colored card stock with glue or transparent tape to fix your pictures in place.

DAFFODIL BUNTING

WELCOME THE SPRING into your home and create some cheery daffodil bunting.

MATERIALS

- Pencil
- Card stock
- Yellow and orange paints
- Sponge or paintbrush

- Scissors
- Egg cartons
- Craft glue
- String, yarn, or ribbon
- Stapler or transparent tape

Start by looking at some real daffodils with the children, counting the petals and talking about the shapes and patterns.

Draw some daffodil star shapes on card stock and paint your daffodils yellow. You could use a sponge, paintbrush, or even fingers to apply the paint. Cut out your daffodils once the paint has dried. If you use a fairly thin card, the wet paint can make the card warp a little as it dries, giving the daffodils a more three-dimensional shape.

Cut out the craters from some egg cartons to make the trumpets for the daffodil centers and paint them yellow or orange, both inside and out.

Once the trumpets are a dry, glue one to the middle of each daffodil star and leave the daffodils to lie flat until the glue dries. Then attach the daffodils to ribbon, string, or yarn using staples or transparent tape and hang up your bunting to deck your home and welcome spring.

DAFFODIL
PINWHEEL

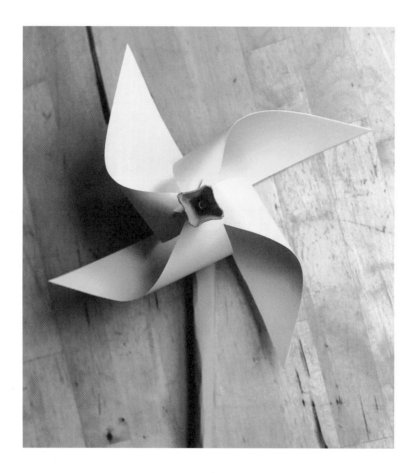

HERE'S A FUN CRAFT that adds a little whizz to your garden.

MATERIALS

- Yellow and green card stock (or white card stock and yellow and green paints)
- Scissors and/or craft knife
- Egg carton
- Paintbrush
- Yellow and/or orange paint
- Pencil
- Ruler
- Transparent tape
- 1-inch brass fastener

Start with a square of yellow card stock. If you are going to paint your card, you will need to cover both sides.

Cut out one of the cup parts of the egg carton—this is going to be the trumpet of your daffodil. Paint it either yellow or orange to be the center of your flower.

Once any paint is dry, draw lines using the ruler on the card as shown and cut along them. Fold in four of the edges. Fasten them in place with a little transparent tape.

Make a stalk for the flower by rolling a piece of the green card into a tube.

Use a brass fastener to join the egg-carton trumpet, the daffodil, and the stalk all together. The fastener should poke straight through the center of the card, but it might be easier to make a hole with either a pencil or a craft knife first. The hole needs to be loose enough for the daffodil to twirl around to give the windmill effect. Then give a gentle blow and watch your daffodil twirl.

LARGE-SCALE
— LANDSCAPE ART —

THE EXTRA SPACE the outdoors offers can translate into art projects too. Take inspiration from the garden and go big and bold and create a huge flower-meadow painting.

MATERIALS

- Long roll of paper
- Fabric and fabric paints (optional)
- Paints
- Sponges
- Leaves
- Paintbrushes
- Pencils
- Flowers

Roll out a long piece of paper—butcher's paper or the reverse side of some wallpaper—and provide a range of painting materials. You can also use a sheet of material and fabric paints to create some art you can hang outside in the garden.

You can do your painting indoors, but if the weather permits, this a wonderful project to take outdoors, so you can paint some of the trees and plants you see around you. The finished artwork is beautiful to display and can also be used as the backdrop for an imaginary play area or puppet theater.

The large scale of this project lends itself well to collaboration, and a family or class can work together, each adding elements to the design. You might use sponges cut into grass and leaf shapes or use real leaves to make prints. Paintbrushes can add stalks. Pencils can sketch flowers before using paint to add color. Use real flowers from the garden to copy, or let your imagination go free.

SPRING FLOWER
BOUQUET

MAKE A MIXED BOUQUET of everlasting flowers to brighten up your table. Here are four design ideas suitable for all ages, so you can pick your favorite or make them all. The four designs are beautiful displayed together in a vase or jug.

EGG-CARTON FLOWERS

Egg-carton flowers are supersimple and great for toddlers and preschoolers who love to paint and sprinkle glitter. To make them, cut out some flower shapes from the craters of the egg cartons. Mix a little glue in with your paint and then put the paint on your flowers. Sprinkle on some glitter and leave the flowers to dry. Make a little hole in the center of your flower and poke a bendy drinking straw or a pipe cleaner through to make your stem.

CUPCAKE-LINER FLOWERS

Cupcake-liner flowers are good for younger children, too, especially fans of glue and glitter. To make them, glue a minicupcake liner inside a bigger one. Choose some colored or patterned cupcake liners or decorate some plain ones. Turn the cupcake liners inside out first to show off the colors and patterns. Add a blob of glue in the center of each flower and around the outer edge, then sprinkle on some glitter. Once they are dry, stick a pipe cleaner or drinking straw on the back with glue or transparent tape to make the stalk.

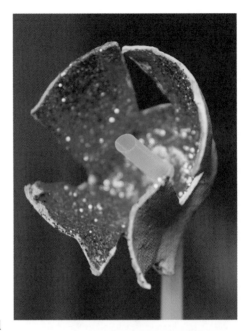

SIMPLE TISSUE-PAPER FLOWERS

This design for tissue-paper flowers is better suited to slightly older children, as toddlers can find it quite tricky to use a finger-and-thumb pincer grip to scrunch up the flowers. To make them, layer three to five squares or circles of tissue paper in matching or contrasting colors. Pinch the center of the tissue papers and scrunch a little to make a flower shape. Use transparent tape to fasten the flower around a bendy drinking straw or a pipe cleaner.

OPULENT TISSUE-PAPER FLOWERS

These tissue-paper flowers are beautiful, full blooms, but they are a bit tricky for younger children, who might find it a little difficult to fold the tissue one way and then the other to make the concertina shape. To make the opulent flowers, layer four rectangular pieces of tissue paper (approximately four inches by twelve inches in size). Fold them in a zigzag, concertina shape starting at a narrow end. Fasten the tissues together around the center with a piece of thread or yarn (or wrap them with your pipe cleaner stalk). Open out the concertina on each side and ruffle up the tissue paper to create the petals.

─ STICKY PICTURES ─

CONTACT PAPER IS A GREAT material to use for children's art, as it allows the children to stick their design in place easily and swap and change things to create new pictures anytime they like. By displaying the pictures within a twig frame, you could make a gallery of these sticky pictures to hang in your garden, against a wall, or from the branches of a tree.

MATERIALS

- 4 twigs
- Yarn or string
- Contact paper
- Thumbtacks or a stapler
- Leaves and petals
- Ribbon

Gather four twigs, all of similar length. Position them in a rectangle and bind the joints with yarn or string.

Peel off the backing from a piece of contact paper and place it sticky side down onto the twig frame. Then fix it in place on the frame with thumbtacks or staples, pushing the thumbtacks into the twigs. Use this as your canvas to create your art. Add leaves and petals from the garden or items from your craft box to create your picture.

Finish off by tying a ribbon around the twigs at the top of the frame so you can hang your picture on display.

CATERPILLARS

PERHAPS THE MOST AMAZING transformation you could study in your garden classroom is the metamorphosis of a caterpillar into a butterfly. There is so much science, beauty, and breathtaking wonder involved. I think children are especially drawn to this, as they can identify with the little caterpillar awaiting and anticipating the change into being grown-up. Here are four ideas for exploring a caterpillar's shape and colors through art, model making, and food.

CATERPILLAR PRINTING

Use various round objects to print with to create a caterpillar. You could use potatoes (with a handle cut out to help little hands), carrots cut in half, and thread spools. Put red paint and shades of green paint into containers for dipping the stamps. Use shades of green to stamp out a caterpillar, overlapping circles along the body. Use red paint to stamp a face. This activity is great for exploring printing and stamping, talking about circles, exploring color shades, and color combining.

JUNK-MODEL CATERPILLAR

To make your junk-model caterpillar, cut out a body from the craters of an egg carton. Provide different shades of green paint and paintbrushes and sponges. Let the children apply the paint to the caterpillar in any pattern they choose (sticking your fingers in the paint is encouraged).

Add a face and finger paint some eyes and a mouth. Two bendy drinking straws make perfect antennae. Use a pencil to poke two holes in the egg carton and insert the drinking straws. You can use your model to act out the story from *The Very Hungry Caterpillar* by Eric Carle. Or take your caterpillar out to the garden for some small-world play and find it a nice green leaf to munch on. This activity is great for using recycled materials, exploring color shades, kids who love painting, working with three dimensions, storytelling with models, and small-world play.

CATERPILLAR COLLAGE

Spread glue in a caterpillar-shaped arch and add lots of small pieces of green paper, combining as many shades, patterns, and textures as you can. Let the children choose which pieces they like best. Add a red face to complete your collage. This activity is great for fine-motor skills, kids who love tearing paper or using scissors, exploring texture, and trying out glue.

A CATERPILLAR YOU CAN EAT

Build an edible caterpillar from cucumber and tomato slices with red pepper antennae and a bed of salad leaves to sit on.

CLOTHESPIN
BUTTERFLY

HERE'S AN IDEA for making a clothespin butterfly using a collage of recycled materials to create the patterns on the wings.

MATERIALS

- Sheet of clear plastic (or card stock or paper)
- Scissors
- Glue
- Embellishments such as recycled paper, tissue paper, tinfoil, sequins, stickers
- Clothespin
- String or yarn
- Pipe cleaner

Take a sheet of clear plastic and cut out a butterfly. (A piece of card stock or paper would work just as well.)

Invite the children to customize the butterfly with liberal amounts of glue, recycled paper, tissue paper, tinfoil, sequins, and stickers. As you make your butterfly, you can talk about symmetry and see if you can get your butterfly's wings to match each other.

Add a line of strong glue down the center of the butterfly and insert the wings into the clothespin. If you want to hang your butterfly, you can tie a length of string or yarn around the pin. Clipping the butterfly to the rim of a drinking glass helps press the wings in place while the glue dries.

Finally, twist a pipe cleaner around the butterfly's head to make the antennae, and draw on a face. Once all the glue is dry, you can hang your butterfly up and watch as the breeze makes it flutter around.

CLAY LEAF
— IMPRESSIONS —

CLAY IS A WONDERFUL MATERIAL to work with in an out-door setting. It's warm, malleable, and natural and can be used in many ways.

Select the type of clay to use depending on the results you want. If you have the facilities, you might like a clay that can be baked or fired. An air-drying clay will dry hard, without baking, in a fairly short amount of time and will work well for this project. Air-drying clay does usually contain nylon, however, so if you are creating your art out in the natural environment, you should look for an all-natural clay that can be left outside to return eventually to the garden ecosystem.

This project takes imprints from some of the natural finds in the garden and preserves them in a tile, which you can use as coasters or pot stands or display on the wall.

MATERIALS

- Leaves, flowers, twigs, or feathers
- Sheet of plastic
- Rolling pin
- Clay
- Pencil
- String, or felt with an adhesive backing (or use glue)
- Paint varnish (optional)

Begin by selecting some items from around the garden that you would like to use in your art: leaves, flowers, twigs, or feathers.

Use the sheet of plastic on a table to create your tile on, making it easy to move and store while you wait for the clay to dry. Roll out some clay into whatever shape of tile you would like to make: a circle, square, or rectangle.

Use the found items to make imprints in the clay. You might like to pick just a single leaf to press into one tile, or maybe you'll want to overlap leaves, flowers, and twigs to create a montage. Remove the items to leave a print in the tile.

If you would like to hang your artwork, make two holes with a pencil at the top of your tile so you will be able to attach some string later. Then leave your tile flat on the plastic sheet to dry. Once the tile is hard, you can add string to hang it, or stick felt on the back if you are going to use it as a coaster or a pot stand. You can add paint or varnish, as desired.

CLAY FACES AND CREATURES

IN THIS PROJECT we use clay to create sculptures against the bark of a tree or on a garden wall. You might like to make an animal or a clay face, such as a Green Man. A Green Man is a symbol found in many cultures around the world, often symbolizing spring, rebirth, the power of nature, and growth.

MATERIALS

- Found items from the garden: leaves, twigs, seeds, flowers
- Natural-based clay

Decide whether you are going to pick items from the plants in your garden or just use things that have already fallen to the ground. Then go on a hunt to see what items you can find that can be used to decorate your character.

Knead your clay a little to form a lump and then slap it against the surface where you are going to create a sculpture. You can use a tree trunk or a wall, but a surface with some texture is best, as the clay will adhere better to a surface that is not too smooth.

Then you are ready to create your face or animal. You can shape the clay to give your face contours, to make a nose or eyes. You can use twigs to draw in the clay and make patterns. You can use the natural materials to add decorations and features.

You can leave your sculpture on your tree or fence as an outdoor art gallery. Take a photograph to include in your garden journal.

— LAND-ART WREATH —

YOU CAN MAKE garden wreaths throughout the year to celebrate the changing seasons. It's a beautiful way to combine a treasure hunt, nature study, and some sculpture.

MATERIALS

- Circular frame for your wreath (see suggestions below)
- Leaves, flowers, and berries
- String, ribbon, or glue

Start by deciding on the frame for your wreath. You might use loops of willow cane, plaited or twined plant stalks, sticks glued or tied together, or a paper plate.

Head out to see what materials you can find to decorate your wreath. This allows you to see what is growing at any particular time of year and use these materials to make your wreath reflect the beauty of the season. Decide whether the children are allowed to pick items that are growing or whether they should gather things only from the garden floor. Once you have a selection of materials, it's time to decorate the wreath. You can poke your found treasures through the wreath frame or use string, ribbon, or glue to hold them in place. Add a ribbon in a festive color at the top of the wreath and hang it up for all to see—on a garden gate, on the door of your shed, at the entrance to your classroom, or above your nature-investigation table. Every child in your class could make a wreath to add to a collaborative celebration of beauty of the time of year.

LAND-ART
MANDALA

MANDALAS ARE TRADITIONAL circular designs used as spiritual or religious symbols in Hinduism and Buddhism. They represent the universe and can be a focus of meditation. This garden-art mandala takes inspiration from land art and Indian mandalas. It explores patterning and symmetry as well as creating beautiful designs that can be temporary or permanent features in the garden. Creating a land-art mandala in your garden is a wonderful way for your children to collaborate on an outdoor art installation.

MATERIALS

- Found items from around the garden: flowers, petals, leaves, sticks, seed heads, feathers, berries

To make a mandala, use your collected materials to create a circular design. You might like to start at the center and work outward, adding layer upon layer to your picture, or you may prefer to define the size of your mandala with an outer layer that you can then fill in. The children might each like to create his or her own mandala, or they may want to work together to complete a joint design.

You might like to try to make your mandala with a line of symmetry running through the center, or to run rings of repeating patterns around it. You can include as many different colors from your garden leaves and petals as you like. Be sure to take some photographs of your finished mandalas to include in your garden journals.

MAKE A
SCARECROW

A SCARECROW IS an iconic figure in a garden, adding stature and sculpture and perhaps even doing its job of keeping birds off your precious seeds and emerging shoots. You don't need to stick with a traditional old-man version though. Use your imagination and create a scarecrow with a dash of style.

MATERIALS

- 2 garden poles
- Twine
- Old clothes and accessories
- Old pillowcase or other fabric sack

- Safety pins
- Needle and thread
- Buttons, scraps of fabric, fabric glue (optional)
- Yarn

Use two garden poles to make a cross, held together with twine. This gives you the basic body, head, and arms. You can choose the size of the poles depending on how big you'd like your finished scarecrow to be. Make sure there is enough length on the body section to push the "feet" partway down into the soil of your vegetable patch to secure your scarecrow in place.

Next, dress your scarecrow. It's great fun to create an out-of-the-ordinary scarecrow, perhaps in a fancy costume resembling a famous person or perhaps copying a character out of a favorite storybook. We used my daughters' old clothes to create our glamorous Cindy Lou. Place the clothes over the garden poles, threading the arms through the sleeves of your outfit. We used old clothes to fill out stockings and tied string around them, which we then hung over the arm poles to position the legs in the right place under the skirt. We "dressed" the stockings with a skirt, held in place with safety pins. To make your scarecrow's face, you can use an old pillowcase. You can stitch on eyes, nose, and mouth with thread; use buttons; or cut out pieces of fabric and attach them with fabric glue. For hair, use yarn or string and attach it in place with a few stitches. You can add any extra embellishments you like: hats, scarves, jewelry, props. Just make sure that whatever you use can cope with being outside in all weather.

A quirky scarecrow adds a touch of humor to your garden, making people smile as they enter it, and it provides a little architectural structure right through the year, even before your plants have matured.

You could even host a scarecrow competition and invite each class in your school or each family in your community to create their own eccentric version.

Yummy
ALLOTMENT RELISH

courgettes, apples, peppers and
onion, with ginger, garlic and a
little chilli

GARDEN
RECIPES

THE TRADITIONAL HIGH POINT of the growing year is the late-summer gathering and celebration of the crops that have been grown. Thanksgiving, Harvest Moon, the Celtic Lughnasa, and other harvest festivals all revolve around a celebration of homegrown food. After your children have been involved in sowing seeds, nurturing plants, and picking the produce they have grown, cooking with the produce completes the cycle of the year.

There is much pride and enjoyment to be had from picking, preparing, and feasting on food *you* have grown. However big or small your garden, there is always space for growing food—whether it is a raised bed full of vegetables, a pot of herbs, or a window box of lettuces. It's so satisfying to grow your own food, harvest it, and eat it right from outside your back door. And by doing this you are letting your children see where their food really comes from—not from a store but out of the soil. Harvesting a crop of tomatoes we have tended, watered, and protected from pests gives a better appreciation of the food we have on our table. And you may find that children who are picky eaters are much more adventurous and open to trying foods if they have had a hand in growing them.

Here are some simple, tasty recipes you can try with your garden harvest, including soup for a shared meal and a relish that's great for using up a glut of summer produce, plus ideas for making great use of herbs and edible flowers all year-round.

of your own herbs and vegetables, they can pick the ingredients right from the garden.

The special thing about this vegetable soup recipe is that there isn't really a recipe at all—just suggestions for children to help them create a signature dish of their own. Whatever combination of vegetables they choose, a ratio of around a total of ten veggies to two pints stock is a rough guide—but have some extra stock ready just in case you need it. A combination of one onion, some garlic, two celery sticks, half a bulb of fennel, three carrots, three parsnips, and one sweet potato, together with two pints of chicken stock, is a good starting point, which will make enough for eight servings.

GARDEN SOUP BASIC PRINCIPLES

Fry some base vegetables in oil in a really big pan: onions, garlic, celery.

Peel and chop some root vegetables and add them to the pan: potato, carrots, sweet potato, parsnips, rutabaga, and fennel are all good. Use a child-friendly peeler to make it easier, and don't worry too much about all the vegetables' being chopped to the same size.

Add some herbs for extra flavor: take your pick from cumin, coriander, oregano, thyme, caraway, parsley, or rosemary.

Add chicken, turkey, or vegetable stock to cover the vegetables and simmer away for about twenty to thirty minutes.

Once the vegetables are soft, you can blend the soup, adding more stock or water, if you like, to get the thickness you prefer.

Serve your customized garden soup with Parmesan cheese and pine nuts on top. The soup freezes really well too.

BASIL PESTO

THIS SIMPLE BASIL PESTO is a great beginner recipe that children can make themselves—with a little adult supervision. It's delicious spread on toasted bread or pizzas, with mashed potatoes, or stirred through pasta.

INGREDIENTS

- 1 handful pine nuts
- 4 child-size handfuls freshly picked basil leaves
- 1 handful freshly grated Parmesan cheese
- 1 glug olive oil
- 1 squeeze lemon juice
- Salt and pepper

Start by toasting the pine nuts in a dry frying pan (no oil added) to give extra flavor. Then simply combine the pine nuts, basil, cheese, and oil in a blender and whizz it all up. You can make the pesto with a pestle and mortar, too, if you don't want the children to use a blender.

Encourage the children's confidence in the kitchen by letting them taste the result and decide for themselves if the sauce needs tweaking with an extra glug of oil or a squeeze of lemon or a bit of salt and pepper.

MORE WAYS TO USE HERBS
FROM YOUR GARDEN

- Snip chives and mix them with smoked mackerel and cream cheese to make a delicious pâté, or add them to scrambled eggs or omelets.
- Sage works perfectly with sausages—try some homemade sausage rolls made by adding chopped sage to sausage meat and folding it inside a puff pastry casing.
- Oregano can be picked, washed, and sprinkled straight onto your pizza.
- Include some lavender stalks under the running water when you fill your bath.
- Use fresh mint leaves to make tea.
- And you can also add chopped herbs to homemade playdough for some garden sensory play.

— ZUCCHINI RELISH —

THIS RECIPE IS a delicious way to use up a glut of zucchini, and it makes a lovely garden gift for others. It's also a great product to sell as a fund-raiser for your garden-classroom project. It has a sweet taste that goes very well with cheese, ham, and burgers.

INGREDIENTS

- 1 large zucchini
- 2 apples
- 1 onion
- 1 sweet pepper
- 1 celery stick
- 1 garlic clove
- 1¼ cups brown sugar
- 1 cup white wine vinegar
- 1 teaspoon ground ginger
- 1 tablespoon mustard
- 1 teaspoon chili powder (mild or strong, to taste)
- ½ teaspoon salt

Peel the zucchini and remove any large seeds, then chop it into small pieces. Peel and core the apples and chop them into small pieces. Chop the onion, pepper, celery, and garlic.

Place the chopped foods and the remaining ingredients in a large pan. Bring the mixture to a boil, then reduce the heat and let the relish simmer, uncovered, until it thickens–about 45 to 60 minutes.

Ladle the relish into sterilized jars, add a lid, and leave the jars to cool. The children can design labels to go on the relish jars, giving them a stylish finish.

GARDEN JOURNAL

Use these pages to get a jump start on your own garden journal. Photocopy these pages or go to www.nurturestore.co.uk/the-garden-classroom or roostbooks.com/thegardenclassroom to download a PDF of these pages and print as many copies as you wish for all the children you are growing with.

MY GARDEN JOURNAL

Writing, observations, and artwork by _____

Date my journal begins _____

TODAY WE PLANTED

Date _____

_____

_____

_____

GARDEN CHORES FOR TODAY

Date _____

_____

_____

_____

TODAY IN THE GARDEN

Date _____

I can see _____

I can hear _____

I can smell _____

I can touch _____

I can taste _____

THREE ORDINARY THINGS I SAW
IN MY GARDEN TODAY

Date _____

1. _____

2. _____

3. _____

THREE EXTRAORDINARY THINGS I SAW
IN MY GARDEN TODAY

Date _____

1. _____

2. _____

3. _____

TODAY IN THE GARDEN

Date _____

_____

_____

_____

QUICK WORD-ASSOCIATION LIST

Leaf _____

Sunshine _____

Flower _____

Growth _____

Bird _____

Harvest _____

Soil _____

Bee _____

Rain _____

Butterfly _____

LIST OF CREATURES THAT LIVE IN MY GARDEN

Date _____

_____

_____

_____

_____

_____

_____

A LIST OF EVERYTHING I CAN HEAR IN THE GARDEN TODAY

Date _____

1. _____

2. _____

3. _____

4. _____

5. _____

6. _____

7. _____

8. _____

9. _____

10. _____

GRAPHING MY GARDEN

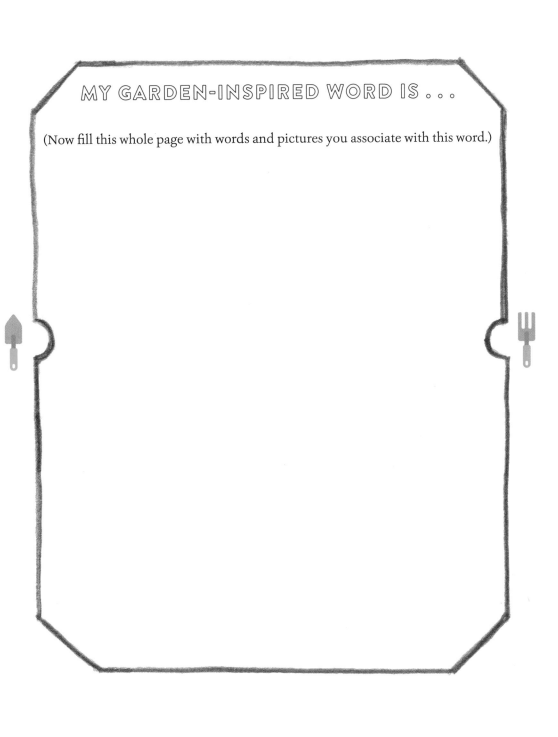

MY GARDEN-INSPIRED WORD IS . . .

(Now fill this whole page with words and pictures you associate with this word.)

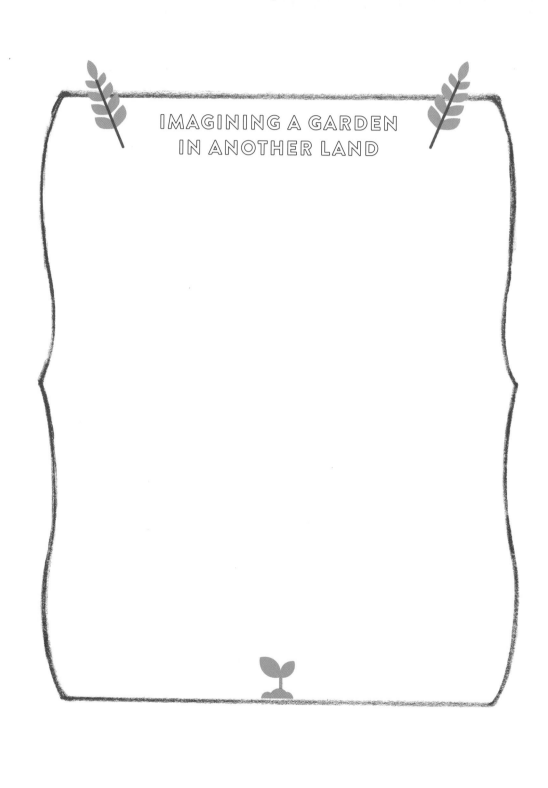

IMAGINING A GARDEN
IN ANOTHER LAND

PLANT OBSERVATION

Date _____

Date _____

Date _____

Date _____

Date _____

Date _____

Date _____

Date _____

RECORD OF ALL THE PRODUCE FROM OUR GARDEN

SCIENCE IN MY GARDEN

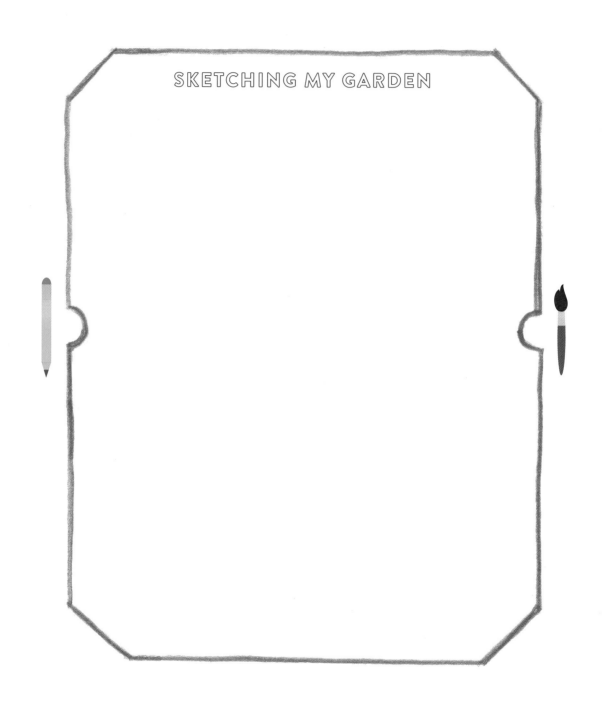

SKETCHING MY GARDEN

A SNAPSHOT OF THE GARDEN TODAY

Ready to pick . . .

The weather is . . .

Growing well . . .

Animals I saw . . .

My favorite thing . . .

What I heard . . .

Something new I noticed today . . .

THINGS I KNOW ABOUT THE GARDEN

Things I know about...

Things I know about...

Things I know about...

Things I know about...

RESOURCES

BLOGS ABOUT CHILDREN'S GARDENING AND OUTDOOR PLAY AND LEARNING

NurtureStore: www.nurturestore.co.uk

Sun Hats and Wellie Boots: www.sunhatsandwellieboots.com

Fantastic Fun and Learning: www.fantasticfunandlearning.com

Happy Hooligans: www.happyhooligans.ca

Let the Children Play: www.letthechildrenplay.net

Go Explore Nature: www.goexplorenature.com

Little Eco Footprints: www.littleecofootprints.com

WEBSITES

The New York Botanical Garden: www.nybg.org/edu/school.php

Creative Star Learning: www.creativestarlearning.co.uk

Royal Horticultural Society: www.rhs.org.uk

Growing Schools: www.growingschools.org.uk

The Growing Schools Garden: www.thegrowingschoolsgarden.org.uk

Garden Organic: www.gardenorganic.org.uk

Gardener's World: www.gardenersworld.com

The National Gardening Association: www.garden.org

GOOD READS FOR ADULTS

The New Vegetable and Herb Expert, D. G. Hessayon

Practical Allotment Gardening, Caroline Foley

The Allotment Book, Andi Clevely

The Therapeutic Garden, Donald Norfolk

Last Child in the Woods, Richard Louv

National Gardening Association Guide to Kids' Gardening, Lynn Ocone

GOOD READS FOR CHILDREN: INFORMATION BOOKS

How a Seed Grows, Helene J. Jordan

From Caterpillar to Butterfly, April McCroskie, ed.

100 Things to Spot in the Garden, Simon Tudhope

The Usborne Big Book of Big Bugs, Usborne Publishing Ltd

The Global Garden, Kate Petty

It's Our Garden: From Seed to Harvest in a School Garden, George Ancona

Our Organic Garden, Precious McKenzie

Kids in the Garden: Growing Plants for Food and Fun, Elizabeth McCorquodale

GOOD READS FOR CHILDREN: PICTURE BOOKS

The Very Hungry Caterpillar, Eric Carle

The King of Tiny Things, Jeanne Willis

Isabella's Garden, Glenda Millard

Quiet in the Garden, Aliki

A Little Yellow Leaf, Carin Berger

Oliver's Vegetables, Vivian French

Flower Garden, Eve Bunting

A Tree Is Nice, Janice May Udry

Heroes of the Vegetable Patch, Ulf Stark

The Listening Walk, Paul Showers

Eddie's Garden and How to Make Things Grow, Sarah Garland

Planting a Rainbow, Lois Ehlert

The Curious Garden, Peter Brown

Outside Your Window: A First Book of Nature, Nicola Davies

Snail Trail, Ruth Brown

Butterfly Butterfly, Petr Horacek

Grandpa's Garden, Stella Fry

To Be Like the Sun, Susan Marie Swanson

The Complete Brambly Hedge, Jill Barklem

The Beatrix Potter Collection, Beatrix Potter
Caterpillar Butterfly, Vivian French
Linnea in Monet's Garden, Christina Bjork
Owl Moon, Jane Yolen

GOOD READS FOR CHILDREN: CHAPTER BOOKS

Lob, Linda Newbery
The Secret Garden, Frances Hodgson Burnett
The Wind in the Willows, Kenneth Grahame
Tom's Midnight Garden, Philippa Pearce

JOIN THE GARDEN CLASSROOM COMMUNITY

If you've enjoyed the ideas in this book, I think you will love my website *NurtureStore*, which is packed full of ideas for children's learning. You'll find more ideas for garden-classroom projects there as well as ideas for math, literacy, art, science, and more. All the activities are based on the belief that children learn best through a playful, multisensory approach. You can also sign up for a free Play Planner e-newsletter, which will deliver a weekly injection of fun play ideas for your children. Come and visit!

www.nurturestore.co.uk

You'll also find a wonderful community of like-minded parents and educators at *NurtureStore*'s Facebook page. It's a great place to swap ideas, find support, and see what play-based learning is going on around the globe. You can find it here:

www.facebook.com/NurtureStore

And for more inspiration, I also curate a number of idea boards on Pinterest, including one specifically dedicated to garden-classroom ideas. Come and follow me on Pinterest and I'll keep you supplied with wonderful, seasonal activities to enjoy.

www.pinterest.com/cathyjames/

ABOUT THE AUTHOR

Cathy James is a mother of two daughters and lives in the United Kingdom. She writes the children's resource blog *NurtureStore,* which is packed full of more than one thousand activities for kids, including play ideas, arts and crafts, math, science, and literacy ideas. Cathy is passionate about learning through creative play and giving children a strong connection with nature. She previously ran a school gardening club and now homeschools her children, where many days are spent learning in the family's organic garden.